THE COMPLETE
QUINOA
COOKBOOK

THE COMPLETE
QUINOA
COOKBOOK

CATHERINE GILL

THE COMPLETE QUINOA COOKBOOK

Text copyright © 2021 Catherine Gill

Library of Congress Cataloging-in-Publication Data
is available upon request.
ISBN: 978-1-57826-883-2

COVER AND INTERIOR DESIGN BY CAROLYN KASPER

FOOD STYLING AND PHOTOGRAPHY BY
CATHERINE GILL AND JASON GILL

ADDITIONAL PHOTOGRAPHY PROVIDED BY
COURTNEY WADE, CATARINA ASTROM,
AND NICHOLE DANDREA-RUSSERT

Printed in the United States
10 9 8 7 6 5 4 3 2 1

This is dedicated to all those affected by the global pandemic, and to those we have lost.

Also, a special thank you to all the first responders and those who continue to work and keep the world moving for all of us.

CONTENTS

PREFACE

AFTER MAKING THE decision to become vegan, one of your first major goals is usually to find suitable, nutritious substitutions for the foods you used to eat. Yet all too often, we find our selection limited—either by what's physically available in our area, or by a scarcity of vegan-friendly alternatives. Which is why, when I first became vegan, I was ecstatic to discover quinoa—a truly protein-packed little seed with all the characteristics and textures of a grain, that can act in a very rice-like way in oh-so-many recipes.

Whether you're a vegan, a vegetarian, a health enthusiast or just someone looking to partake in meatless meals whenever possible, you owe it to yourself to explore everything that quinoa has to offer. As I've been experimenting with quinoa over the years, I'm constantly impressed by its versatility and sheer ease of use. Recipes like rice pudding, veggie burgers, stuffed peppers, and a great many more—all using this fluffy seed, which has an even better nutritional profile than a lot of the foods that we are accustomed to using. In fact, quinoa is one of the most nutrient dense superfoods around.

I quickly set out to become unstoppable, creating as many dishes as I could with quinoa in them. and now, naturally, I want to share these revelations with the world! In the same way I worked to bring *The Dirty Vegan Cookbook* and *The Complete Hummus Cookbook*, now *The Complete Quinoa Cookbook* is available to you to completely change what goes on in your kitchen. The goal of these books has always been to provide readers with a way to broaden their culinary horizons while at the same time satisfying both their health *and* their taste buds. Whether it is breakfast, lunch, dinner, snacks, desserts, or something else, this book and its recipes have your quinoa curiosities covered.

In earning my certification as a vegan nutrition health coach, I have really grown to understand the magic of quinoa in the way that it rises to meet your body's nutrition needs. Drawing on my experiences as a holistic chef and a vegan nutrition health coach, I am proud to present you with this cookbook: a medley of food art as well as sound, healthful meals created to support your wellness. As in my other works, I have also included a fun history of quinoa, useful tips and fascinating facts—you'll see, this book really does live up to its name as truly being *The Complete Quinoa Cookbook!*

Now, let's dive in and learn about this tiny—but profound—little seed that we call quinoa!

Peace and love,

Catherine

WHAT IS QUINOA?

YOU SAY YOU'VE never heard of quinoa? I find that a bit hard to believe, but hey, perhaps you picked up this book not knowing anything about it. Kudos to you, then, for expanding your horizons!

Let's start with the pronunciation of quinoa. Over the years, I have heard many people pronounce it many different ways and have received lots of questions from readers asking, "How on earth do I pronounce this word?" The official pronunciation…is *KEEN-waa*.

I know, right? That one comes as quite the shock to most people. Don't worry—I was completely mispronouncing it, too, but I'm grateful to now know the correct pronunciation, so that next time I am at a hip vegan restaurant ordering a Buddha bowl and I'm asked if I want brown rice or quinoa, I won't sound like a complete and utter square.

But where did quinoa come from? Who discovered it? What region does it originate from? How did people use it back then? We all know that foods and ingredients evolve over time and from place to place; as food is traded and introduced to various countries, it is prepared in brand new ways (how exciting!). So, in my pursuit of becoming a queen of quinoa, I immersed myself in my quinoa research—I just wanted to know everything about it.

A BRIEF HISTORY OF QUINOA

Quinoa originated as an Andean plant in Peru and Bolivia, in the surrounding Lake Titicaca area. Originally cultivated by the pre-Columbian civilizations, quinoa was used in more types of breakfast cuisine at first, but was eventually replaced by prepared cereals after the arrival of Spanish conquistadors. It was considered a staple food in the local community at the time prior to the 16th century. Historical evidence exists which hints that the people of America may have begun domestication of quinoa sometime between 3,000 to 5,000 BCE. However, archeological findings have discovered quinoa in tombs found in Tarapaca and other regions in Chile, and various Peruvian regions.

While the discoverer of quinoa (likely a native of the land quinoa was originally sowed on) is unknown, one Spaniard keeps cropping up when talking about quinoa's history. Long after the grain-like seed's crops had already been well-cultivated and widely circulated in societal, cultural and economic existence, Pedro de Valdivia made journal notes during his exploration indicating that this crop had been in existence and cultivated by the natives in the Concepcion area. So, while Pedro de Valdivia is not the one who discovered quinoa himself, he appears to be the first person to ever put anything about quinoa in writing.

The next famous publication to mention quinoa was by Garcilaso de la Vega in 1906. Garcilaso de la Vega was the first published mestizo writer of colonial Andean South America and was author of the *Royal Commentaries of the Incas*. In his book, quinoa is described as the second-most cultivated grain on the earth, next to either rice or millet. This tells us that even with limited food technology available, quinoa was still thought of as a grain instead of a seed. Garcilaso de la Vega also wrote about the shipping, transport and germination process of the seeds, but still ultimately referred to quinoa as a grain.

Mentions of quinoa in the historical record become more frequent from this point; for example, Pedro Cieza de León, a Spanish conquistador and noted chronicler of the history of Peru, describes the abundance of quinoa that was found growing in the highlands and cold lands of the Peruvian regions. Quinoa is also cited by him as an abundant food grown by indigenous people, one which was used whole, leaves and seeds.

As quinoa began to be grown and harvested in different parts of the world, it changed in size, started to vary in shape, and even the colors and ways the seeds are dispersed diverged from that of the original crop. This abundance of variety has

continued to this day: quinoa can be toasted, used as flour, soups and stews, and more. The various types of quinoa are used in different regions and in certain dishes, according to their resiliency and yield. For instance, "chullpi" quinoa (not to be confused with chulpi toasted corn) is a quinoa which holds up nicely for use in stews or soups. "Coytos" quinoa is a good flour substitute due to its texture. "Pissara", which many people know as the lighter-colored quinoa, is used as a rice substitute. "Ayaras" quinoa is one known for its nutrition density, as it is high in balanced protein and essential amino acids, making it a perfect protein that your body can use for fuel right away.

Of course, this is barely scratching the surface of quinoa's varieties. Let's take a closer look at all the options afforded by what the ancient Incas called "the Mother Grain."

DIFFERENT TYPES OF QUINOA

Did you know that there are over 100 types of quinoa? Yes, *one hundred*. Wow! Of course, you'd be hard-pressed to find a store carrying all 100 varieties. The most common types that you may have seen at your grocery store, seen prepared at a restaurant, or have cooked at home will be black, red, and white quinoa.

Black quinoa is a sweeter tasting quinoa and has an earthy flavor to it. It is tender when cooked and has a nutty flavor and quality to it. Black quinoa transforms from a solid black color to a lighter color with a deep brown hue. Black quinoa is my favorite variety to use, especially when baking, because it works well in baked goods and looks beautiful. Black quinoa also makes for the choice for use in side dishes.

Red quinoa is the type you'll commonly see in restaurant salads and Buddha or vegetable bowls. This type of quinoa can hold its shape when mixed with other ingredients, as red quinoa does not get as mushy or starchy the way white quinoa or rice does. Red quinoa remains hard and firm even after cooking, and the texture is very complementary in salad bowls.

White quinoa is the most popular type that is easily found at supermarkets and is frequently served in eateries. It is commonly used because of its tenderness when cooked and a fluffiness that is similar to white rice. When white quinoa is popped, it resembles a tiny kernel of popcorn, so it is often used in health foods, popped quinoa bars, cookies and other prepackaged foods, as well as in an array of healthy candies. Popped white quinoa is very popularly seen in vegan chocolate varieties like bars, truffles, or chocolate barks.

Another reason why white quinoa is such high demand is because it is the type of quinoa used in puffed quinoa. Puffed quinoa is the results of commercial puffing and is nearly identical to the process used to make puffed rice cereal. You can purchase puffed quinoa in bags, just like crispy, puffed rice cereal, which can be used it in many of the recipes you will find later in this book. Puffed quinoa can also be made at home, although it does not quite come out the same as the commercially made variety; we simply do not have access to the same food manufacturing machinery that quinoa food producers do. If you are

looking for that same texture and consistency that puffed quinoa has to offer, you will have to purchase it from your local health food store.

As a side note, there is also tricolored quinoa and quinoa mixtures that include several types of quinoa in one bag. These mixtures provide decent options for when you like to have different flavors and consistencies in one bite and can make your dishes more interesting, too.

PREPARING QUINOA

Speaking of different types of quinoa! There are nearly as many ways to prepare quinoa as there are different varieties! The most popular versions are cooked, popped, toasted and puffed, and ground (for the purpose of using as flour). You can also boil quinoa in water, vegetable or other liquid stocks, or vegan milks.

The general rule when cooking quinoa is the double ratio. If you are cooking 1 cup of dry quinoa, you will want to use 2 cups of liquid. You will also want to rinse any quinoa before use unless the package specifies that it has been pre-rinsed. (Some quinoa instructions may ask you to soak, but a quick rinse is usually all it takes.) This is because quinoa is naturally coated in a bitter tasting substance called saponin. If

you have ever tasted quinoa with a lot of bitterness, chances are it was not rinsed sufficiently.

Once the liquid is brought to a boil, reduce the heat and let it gently simmer. The quinoa will absorb the liquid and be ready in about 20 minutes time. Once all the liquid is absorbed, you will want to fluff your quinoa with a fork. And that's it! That is all that needs to be done; like rice, quinoa absorbs the liquid so well that using a flavored broth and adding seasonings to it is enough to make a nice treat with extremely tasty results.

Toasted or popped quinoa is one of my favorite ways to prepare it. As you will notice in many of the recipes in this cookbook, you pop your own quinoa by warming a pan with oil (or toast in a skillet), usually olive oil or coconut, and heating the quinoa seeds.

Ground quinoa is used as flour and has been for centuries, likely ground using a mortar and pestle or similar hand grinding tools. Today, we are lucky to have food processors that make short work of processing your own quinoa flour: just process in a blender or food processor and you will have a fine powder. Quinoa flours work in combination with all-purpose flour or with other flours like bread flour and gluten-free flour. You will notice quinoa flour also responds well to leavening agents like baking soda and baking flour, which are substances that cause dough to expand when baked.

QUINOA'S NUTRITION

The best part about quinoa is eating it, obviously—it truly is a culinary superstar. But did you know that it is also very nutritious? This is due to quinoa's unique nature as a grain-like seed, so you're getting the best of both worlds here. It provides the protein and amino benefits of a seed, while taking on the textures, appearances and uses that a grain would.

Unlike some other seeds, quinoa can absorb water much like a grain. Depending on the variety of quinoa, it can range in its nutritional value, but on average it contains all nine essential amino acids (yay for perfect protein!), and has around 5 grams of fiber and 8 grams of protein per one cooked cup. Quinoa is low in saturated fat, is cholesterol-free (as all vegan, non-animal foods are), high in fiber, and naturally low in sodium. Quinoa is also typically gluten-free, so long as there is no cross contamination and the product's packaging states that it is certified gluten-free and made in a facility free of gluten contaminates. In addition, quinoa also contains vitamins B 1, 2, 3, 6 and 9, and vitamin E. Quinoa is also an excellent source of minerals like copper, phosphorus, zinc, iron, selenium, potassium, and calcium. In fact, 51 percent of an average person's daily value of manganese and 28% of magnesium per one cup cooked serving.

ENVIRONMENTAL RESPONSIBILITY AND QUINOA

It is more important than ever that we act responsibly as aware, conscious consumers who are mindful of the problems facing the world and the environment today. In regards to quinoa, that means it is imperative we purchase only high-quality, ethically and environmentally responsible products from companies who do not use harmful toxic chemical fertilizers that can harm the plant and its ecosystem. These chemicals, which can seep into the water and soil causing long-term damage, can also be detrimental to human health.

Look for companies who abide by the highest standards and acknowledge this problem while demonstrating what they are doing to avoid adding to that dilemma. All it takes is a quick phone call, letter, or e-mail to a company to find out how it produces and harvests its quinoa. There is typically also information available on a brand's website, so take a look for yourself before making your purchasing decisions. A general rule of thumb you may want to try is to patronize brands that you trust with good quality ingredients and honest practices. There is power in being a consumer, so spend your money where your values also reside!

It is also a good idea to always purchase certified organic products when at all possible and do your best research on what exactly you are purchasing and where it comes from. This may take a little extra effort, but you get to rest easy in the knowledge that where you put your money is contributing as little as possible to negative environmental or moral consequences. It is always freeing to be able to make and enjoy delicious recipes, but they'll taste twice as good with a clean conscience. Knowing you are contributing positivity and good to this world, as much as you can, is just as good for you as quinoa!

THE RECIPES

BREAKFAST

★

THESE DAYS, QUINOA might seem a rather unlikely or even unusual breakfast ingredient, but rest assured, it was a breakfast staple long ago and still makes for a great start to the day even now! While we might not often think of using quinoa as a go-to for our first meal of the day, it is a wonderful and powerfully nutritious way to kick off the day's events. Being rich in nutrients and providing slow-releasing energy, quinoa is a delicious and easily digestible item to add to your morning dishes.

You will find the following recipes not only satisfy your taste buds, but also offer healthful alternatives to fast digesting carbs which could never hold you over until the next meal the way quinoa can.

CHOCOLATE STRAWBERRY QUINOA BREAKFAST BOWL

Serves 1

1 cup prepared vegan yogurt

½ cup strawberries

½ cup quinoa, cooked and cooled

1 tablespoon vegan chocolate or cacao chips

1 tablespoon pepitas

1 tablespoon chia seeds

1 tablespoon pure maple syrup (optional)

Cinnamon, to taste

Nutmeg, to taste

It only makes sense to add a superfood like quinoa to your breakfast routine. A complete protein, this tiny seed packs a powerful health punch and is a perfect start to your busy day, while still giving you the comforting feeling of eating a "grain." You will find this nutritious morning bowl refreshing *and* satisfying.

In a serving or soup bowl, add ingredients in an aesthetically pleasing way. You may serve right away, or cover and refrigerate overnight, to serve the next morning.

Tip: Breakfast bowls are not just convenient but also extremely customizable. Feel free to use this recipe as a base or starting point and add or change up the topics according to your preference. Some other excellent topic choices include sprinkling on some shredded coconut, stirring in some nut or seed butters, and changing up the fruit seasonally. You might find that a morning or snack bowl like this, will become a lovely new part of your routine.

QUINOA MUFFINS

Serves 12

¼ cup olive oil

2 ripe bananas, peeled and mashed

½ cup cooked quinoa, any type

¼ cup pure maple syrup

1 teaspoon pure vanilla extract

2 apples, cored and shredded

3–4 carrots, shredded

½ cup soy milk

½ teaspoon sea salt

1½ teaspoon baking soda

½ teaspoon ground cinnamon

⅛ teaspoon ground nutmeg

⅔ cup old fashioned oats

¼ cup wheat germ

1 cup all-purpose flour

¼ cup walnuts, chopped (optional)

This recipe was my take on my classic healthy, rich-in-fiber muffins that I have been enjoying as my breakfast. No matter how many times I make them, everyone enjoys them so much! They are wonderful toasted or warmed with a little bit of vegan butter on them. Once I began making them with quinoa, I loved these muffins just the same as always…plus the added protein and nutrition is a huge bonus!

Preheat oven to 375°F and line a muffin pan with 12 liners or grease cups.

In a medium-sized mixing bowl, combine olive oil, banana mash, quinoa, maple syrup, vanilla extract, shredded apples and carrots, and soy milk, or vegan milk of your choice. In a large mixing bowl, combine dry ingredients, sea salt, baking soda, cinnamon, nutmeg, oats, wheat germ, and flour. Add wet and dry ingredients together and scoop equal amounts of batter into each cup in muffin pan. Lightly press walnuts into the tops of the muffin batter.

Bake for 32–36 minutes or until a toothpick comes out clean. Allow to cool on a wire rack and enjoy slightly warm. Store in an airtight container in the refrigerator for up to one week or freeze for up to one month.

TOFU & QUINOA BREAKFAST SCRAMBLE

Serves 4–6

2 tablespoons extra-virgin olive oil

½ small onion, finely chopped

1 garlic clove, minced

1 (15-ounce) block firm tofu, drained and crumbled

½ cup cooked quinoa, any type

½ teaspoon turmeric powder

Salt and pepper, to taste

Tofu scramble is one of my favorite breakfasts of all time. It is super easy and quickly prepared, and the best part is it's an excellent source of protein. This is a base recipe which tastes amazing simply as-is; however, I like to spice things up by adding different flavors, vegetables, nutritional yeast, and a variety of vegan butters or cheeses. When a hearty morning meal is in order, this recipe is one of my go-to dishes. I am sure it will become a regular in your household breakfast recipe rotation just as it is in my kitchen.

In a large skillet on medium heat, sauté onion and garlic in olive oil until aromas are released. Add tofu and quinoa then sprinkle with turmeric. Cook, stirring frequently, until tofu has browned and scramble is well combined. Season with salt and pepper.

Tip: What I like to do with quinoa is prepare a batch in my rice cooker to include in the weekly meal plan. Quinoa can keep in an airtight container in the refrigerator for a couple days, the same as rice, although I try not to go longer than three days before enjoying it for best freshness and food safety.

QUINWAFFLES

Makes approximately 6 waffles

DRY INGREDIENTS

1½ cups all-purpose flour

¼ teaspoon baking soda

2 teaspoons baking powder

⅛ teaspoon salt

¼ teaspoon cinnamon

¼ teaspoon nutmeg

¼ cup brown sugar

WET INGREDIENTS

2 tablespoons ground flaxseed, mixed with 1 tablespoon water (to be used as egg replacer)

3 tablespoons vegan butter, melted

3 tablespoons coconut oil, melted

1⅓ cup vegan milk

½ cup cooked quinoa, any type

1 ripe banana, mashed

1 teaspoon pure vanilla extract

When writing my books, I always include a contribution from my kiddo. She helps me come up with the idea, as well as helping to write and create the recipes. All my family members are awesome taste testers; it really is a group effort! A big thank you to my wonderful kiddo for coining the term Quinwaffle and helping me with this recipe. You will love the texture that cooked quinoa adds to these waffles when they are prepared, and they are a great, nutritious way to start the day!

Follow your waffle maker manufacturer's instructions to preheat and use your waffle maker. Mix dry ingredients together in one bowl and wet ingredients together in another, separate bowl, before combining both wet and dry ingredients together. Use this batter in your waffle maker, again following the manufacturer's instructions for cooking times. Cooking times will vary, but it is typically 2–4 minutes per waffle to cook them to perfection. Serve with your favorite waffle toppings.

Tip: Excellent waffle toppings include vegan butter, fruit jams or preserves, fresh fruit, non-dairy whipped topping, nut or seed butters, or whatever you can think up!

QUINOA PANCAKES

Makes approximately 6 medium-sized pancakes

1 cup all-purpose flour

1 tablespoon sugar

2 tablespoons
   baking powder

⅛ teaspoon salt

1 cup vegan milk

2 tablespoons extra-virgin
   olive oil

½ cup cooked
   quinoa, any type

When I came up with the idea to use quinoa in pancakes, I wanted to use my same go-to base pancake recipe that has been successful for me for so many years. After making some adjustments to using cooked quinoa in the pancakes, it worked like a charm! Any occasion where you can add more protein and nutrition to your breakfast is a winner to me—and this one tastes amazing to boot!

To prepare, preheat a lightly greased frying pan, skillet, or griddle to medium-high heat. In a mixing bowl, combine flour, sugar, baking powder and salt. Combine milk and olive oil together and add it to dry mixture. Fold in cooked quinoa.

To cook, scoop about ¼ cup of batter and pour onto heated pan or griddle. Let one side of pancake cook until you see bubbles start to form on top, then flip. Pancakes will cook about 3 minutes per side, but the time can vary depending on your cooking device.

Tip: Let your first pancake be your "tester" so you can judge the cooking time for the rest of the batch. Double (or triple) this recipe if serving these pancakes for a crowd.

BERRY, YOGURT & QUINOA PARFAIT

Serves 4

2 cups vegan yogurt,
   any flavor

1 cup cooked
   quinoa, any type

1 cup mixed berries

1 cup granola

1 tablespoon pure
   maple syrup

This breakfast is so easy to put together yet so elegant in appearance! I am always amazed by people's delightful reactions to a dish that was so simple for me to whip up. This is a great breakfast to serve when you are short on time, but still want to make something special.

In four mason jars, parfait glasses or single serving dishes, layer the yogurt, quinoa, and berries. Just before serving, top with granola and drizzle with maple syrup.

Tip: These parfaits can be made the night before. If you are serving overnight guests, consider making them ahead of time for a quick yet impressive breakfast or brunch item.

QUINOA OVERNIGHT OATS

Serves 2

½ cup cooked quinoa, any type

½ cup old fashioned oats

1 ripe banana, peeled and mashed

2 cups vegan milk

¼ teaspoon pure vanilla extract (optional)

¼ teaspoon ground cinnamon (optional)

2 tablespoons toppings (optional)

I made this dish for the first time the night before heading out on a road trip. I had not made this type of overnight oats before, so I was a little unsure about how it was going to turn out, but it sure did fill us up and provide long lasting fuel for our vacationing adventures. I made it in a mason jar and have been doing overnight oats this way, ever since.

In a mixing bowl, add all ingredients then transfer to a container with a lid or other covering. This recipe is for two servings, but you can cut the ingredients in half and prepare directly in your container for easier and quicker preparation. Place jars in the refrigerator overnight and enjoy in the morning. This dish can be stored in the refrigerator for up to five days in advance, but for maximum freshness, I recommend making it the night before, or enjoying your refrigerated quinoa overnight oats within at least three days.

Tip: This meal is very customizable. This is more of a base recipe, so feel free to experiment and have a blast creating in the kitchen using different variations of toppings and changing ingredients. You can add frozen berries on top and wake up to a nice treat. Chocolate chips and nut butters are an excellent option to stir in. Try different milks for a change in creaminess and flavor, or add spices to go with the season. For example, in the late autumn, I made mine gingerbread flavor by using typical flavors one would use in the cookie. Other fun takes on these quinoa overnight oats are: eggnog inspired, pumpkin spice flavored, or anything that you can think up! Just replace some of the banana that the recipe calls for, with organic pumpkin puree, and voila, a hip and trendy breakfast fit for fall.

CHEWY ALMOND QUINOA GRANOLA BARS

Makes 12 bars

1 tablespoon extra-virgin olive oil

¼ cup dry quinoa

2 cups old-fashioned oats

½ cup almonds, chopped

⅔ cup pure maple syrup

¼ cup vegan butter, melted

1 teaspoon pure vanilla extract

These bars remind me of a certain healthy granola bar that I would get at a coffee shop that went excellent with a nice latte or tea. I'd been wanting to recreate something similar for a long time, and so these fantastic bars were born. What's better than getting a little protein in along with your morning cuppa joe?

Line a 9 x 11-inch baking dish with parchment paper. In a medium-sized saucepan on medium heat, heat olive oil and add quinoa. Stir quinoa frequently until all quinoa has popped. Remove quinoa from heat and allow to cool in a bowl.

Mix remaining ingredients into popped quinoa and transfer to baking dish and press firmly. Refrigerate for 2–4 hours, or until bars have set. Cut into 12 evenly sized bars.

Tip: You can keep these bars plain or use this recipe as a base and add ½ cup of chopped chocolate or vegan chocolate chips. You can even add dried fruit like cranberries to it. Be creative!

QUINOA CEREAL & TOPPING

Serves 4–6

¼ cup coconut oil

4 cups dry quinoa

¼ cup vegan butter, melted

¼ cup pure maple syrup

2 tablespoons orange juice

Since quinoa's history has its roots in the cereal indus-try, way back when, it seemed only fitting to create this recipe! Use this in the same way you would use granola or muesli cereal, while adding fresh fruit and a little bit of plant-based milk. You can also top your yogurt with this tasty and crunchy concoction. And for an extra-in-teresting way to make your vegan ice cream or frozen yogurt feel more healthful, use it as a topping on frozen desserts, too!

Preheat oven to 350°F. Lightly grease a large baking sheet.

In a large saucepan, on medium heat, heat coconut oil and add quinoa. Stir quinoa frequently until all quinoa has popped. Transfer quinoa to large mixing bowl and combine popped quinoa with melted butter, maple syrup and orange juice then transfer to baking sheet.

Spread quinoa mixture out evenly on baking sheet and bake for 20 minutes or until lightly browned. Allow to cool before breaking apart. This cereal can be stored in an airtight container for about one week.

Tip: Use this as a cereal similar to granola and enjoy with milk or use as a topping for yogurt or ice cream.

CINNAMON APPLE QUINOA BREAKFAST BOWL

Serves 2

1 tablespoon coconut oil

2 apples, cored
and chopped

1 teaspoon cinnamon

1 tablespoon fresh
lemon juice

2 tablespoons pure
maple syrup

½ cup cooked
quinoa, any type

What a lovely, comforting breakfast bowl to have when you are tired of the typical oatmeal in the morning! The warm cooked apple and cinnamon combined with quinoa provides a nice, cozy feeling. Pairs very well with a nice soothing cup of coffee, tea, or hot cocoa.

In a large saucepan on low heat, melt coconut oil and cook apples until softened. Stirring frequently, add cinnamon, lemon juice and maple syrup; mix well. Fold in the quinoa and continue heating until quinoa is warmed. Transfer to two bowls to serve.

Tip: This is delightful served warm right after preparation, or refrigerated and enjoyed cold with a dollop of vegan whipped topping, as more of a dessert.

QUINOA BISCOTTI

Makes approximately 30 biscotti

1 tablespoon extra-virgin olive oil

¼ cup dry quinoa

4 tablespoons vegan butter

⅔ cup brown sugar

2 teaspoons pure vanilla extract

¼ teaspoon sea salt

2 teaspoons baking powder

2 cups all-purpose flour

½ cup vegan milk

Biscotti is such a perfect breakfast companion to tea or coffee, or even as just a fun snack! I love how portable biscotti is, so if you eat on the run, these make the perfect go-to for busy mornings.

Preheat oven to 350°F. In a medium-sized saucepan on medium heat, heat olive oil and add quinoa. Stir quinoa frequently until all quinoa has popped. Remove quinoa from heat and allow to cool in a bowl and set aside. In a large mixing bowl, cream butter, sugar, and vanilla extract. Mix in dry ingredients, salt, baking powder and flour. Fold in popped quinoa and add in vegan milk until dough batter is sticky in consistency.

Divide dough into two pieces and form into two logs on baking sheet. Bake for 25 minutes then remove from oven and allow biscotti to cool enough to safely handle. Cut biscotti into slices, about 15 pieces per log, then return to the baking sheet and bake slices for an additional 12 minutes per side, for a total of about 24–25 minutes or until biscotti is golden and dry. Allow to cool. Can be stored in an airtight container for about one week.

Tip: You can fold in sliced almonds or press them on top of biscotti dough prior to baking, to make a fancier biscotti variety. Biscotti is excellent for dipping in a warm beverage.

MAPLE QUINOA & TOASTED ALMOND STUFFED CANTALOUPE

Serves 2

1 teaspoon extra-virgin olive oil

¼ cup almonds

1 cup cooked quinoa, any type

3 tablespoons pure maple syrup

2 tablespoons orange juice

½ teaspoon cinnamon

1 cantaloupe, cut in half and seeded

Adding toasted almond to anything is such a treat! This stuffed cantaloupe is no exception. You will love the pleasing and unexpected flavors in each bite as well as the beautiful presentation of this dish.

Preheat oven to 350°F. Lightly oil a baking sheet with olive oil and spread almonds evenly on the sheet. Bake for 10 minutes or until almonds are golden in color and a toasted aroma is released from them. Allow almonds to cool then chop.

In a mixing bowl, combine cooked quinoa, maple syrup, orange juice and cinnamon, then stuff cantaloupe halves with this filling. Top with chopped toasted almonds.

Tip: Don't have almonds but still want to make this recipe? Try using walnuts or pecans!

QUINOA COFFEE CAKE MUFFINS

Serves 12

MUFFINS

1½ cups all-purpose flour

½ cup and 2 tablespoons sugar

½ teaspoon salt

2½ teaspoons baking powder

¼ cup vegetable shortening, softened

½ cup cooked quinoa, any type

¾ cup vegan milk

2 tablespoons ground flaxseed mixed with 1½ tablespoons water

TOPPING

⅓ cup brown sugar

¼ cup all-purpose flour

½ teaspoon cinnamon

3 tablespoons vegan butter

Quinoa is one of those foods that pairs wonderfully with basically anything, but I have noticed it goes particularly nicely with all things cinnamon. These coffee cake muffins, with the addition of moist and nutrition-packed quinoa, is really something special. It is also nice to have coffee cake muffins rather than making an entire coffee cake because muffins are easy to take with you on the go.

Preheat oven to 375°F and prepare a muffin pan by greasing it or lining it with muffin liners. In a large mixing bowl, combine 1½ cups of flour, the sugar, salt, baking powder, shortening, cooked quinoa, milk, and flaxseed with water mixture; mix until thoroughly combined. Evenly distribute batter into the 12 muffin cups.

In a medium mixing bowl, combine brown sugar, ¼ cup flour, cinnamon, and butter until crumbly and well mixed. Sprinkle this topping evenly on top of batter of each muffin cup. Bake for 25 minutes or until a cake tester inserted into the cake comes out cleanly when removed.

Tip: For a fancier appearance, try using different type and colors of quinoa. When you bite into or cut a muffin, you will see the beautiful contrast, of say, red quinoa, to the golden cake in the muffin, and it will make for a lovely presentation.

HEARTY QUINOA TOFU SCRAMBLE
Serves 4–6

2 tablespoons extra-virgin olive oil

½ small onion, finely chopped

1 garlic clove, minced

1 bell pepper, seeded and julienned

1 medium tomato, chopped

1 (15-ounce) block firm tofu, drained and crumbled

½ cup cooked quinoa, any type

½ teaspoon turmeric powder

¾ cup vegan cheese, shredded

1 cup fresh spinach, chopped

⅛ cup fresh basil, chopped

Salt and pepper, to taste

This scramble is similar to my Tofu and Quinoa Breakfast Scramble recipe, but not as simple or quick. This scramble is a heartier version which is more complex and probably better suited for a weekend or for a morning when you have time to prepare all the veggies. Take your time and enjoy making this one!

In a large skillet on medium heat, sauté the onion and garlic in olive oil until aromas are released. Add bell pepper and tomato; cook until peppers are tender. Add tofu and quinoa then sprinkle with turmeric. Add cheese.

Cook, stirring frequently, until tofu has browned, scramble is well combined, and cheese is melted. Turn off heat and add spinach and basil; stir and allow to wilt slightly. Season with salt and pepper to taste.

Tip: This breakfast scramble tastes awesome when served over toasted and buttered fresh bread. This is a wonderful meal for when you are entertaining guests, especially during the holidays.

APPETIZERS AND SNACKS

Q UINOA TAKES THE guesswork out of making today's snacks and lighter meals healthy as well as filling enough to hold you over until the next one. Quinoa doesn't give that bogged down feeling that a huge meal would but provides ample protein and nutrition for those days when you want a lighter lunch or dinner, or a nice lead-in to a meal. This section provides plenty of cool and easy ideas that will satisfy your food cravings between those more formal dishes.

COLORFUL & CRUNCHY QUINOA SLAW SALAD WITH AVOCADO VINAIGRETTE DRESSING

Serves 8–10

2 cups cabbage, shredded

2 cups carrot, shredded

1 medium onion, chopped

1½ cups quinoa, cooked and cooled

¼ cup prepared vegan mayonnaise or oil (like olive or vegetable)

¼ cup avocado, mashed or guacamole

1 tablespoon balsamic vinegar

Salt and pepper, to taste

Quinoa tends to be on the mushier side when cooked, particularly when over-cooked in a boiled fashion. That's why, to make quinoa dishes more interesting in terms of texture, pairing with crisp vegetables is an excellent choice for that crunchy appeal. To make this dish extra-special, get the most beautiful seasonal produce that you can find at your local farmers' market. While this is a dish that looks gorgeous when it is all mixed up together, it is also fun to serve this slaw in a gradient or ombre style, then add your rich colored vinaigrette dressing and toss all together, right in front of your guests for a tasty, visually stimulating treat!

In a large salad bowl or serving dish, combine cabbage, carrot, onion, and quinoa. In a separate bowl or in a food processor, mix mayonnaise, avocado and vinegar to make the dressing. Pour dressing on slaw salad and toss together thoroughly. Season with salt and pepper to taste.

Tip: For more vibrancy, choose different colors of rainbow carrots or onions, cabbage in multiple shades, and quinoa in various hues. By doing so, it can be very visually exciting and impressive, whether you're entertaining or bringing this dish to your next potluck.

QUINOA VEGGIE BURGERS
Serves 4–6

2 tablespoons extra-virgin olive oil

½ cup onion, chopped

1 garlic clove, minced

1 cup frozen mixed vegetables

½ cup water

1 cup cooked quinoa, any type

1 cup breadcrumbs

This veggie burger recipe is easy to customize in many ways: you can make smaller patties and serve them as appetizers or as sliders; you can make them big and serve four nice heavy burgers for a more restaurant style sandwich; you can even choose different veggies to include in your patty mix. It is up to you, so use this as a guide and eventually begin to experiment with different styles and flavors of veggie burgers. Once you start making your own veggie burgers at home, you will wonder why you had not done this all along instead of buying store bought as often.

In a large frying pan or skillet on medium heat, sauté onion and garlic for about 3 minutes. Add mixed vegetables and stir frequently, until very tender. Remove from heat and allow to cool enough to handle safely. In a food processor, blend vegetable mixture and water and transfer to a large mixing bowl.

Combine vegetable mixture, quinoa, and breadcrumbs. The veggie burger mixture should be sticky enough to form patties; if not, add a little more water until desired consistency is achieved. Form into 4–6 evenly-sized and shaped patties. These can also be frozen between wax paper and stored in airtight bags in the freezer for up to one month. Grill, broil, or sauté in pan as you normally would prepare veggie burgers. Sauté on medium heat in lightly oiled pan for 3–5 minutes each side, or until crispy and cooked thoroughly.

Tip: Making a more moist batch of quinoa for this recipe works really well in helping to bind the mixture and help it all stick together. You may need to add some extra water to your patty mixture depending on the climate where you live.

PAN SAUTÉED QUINOA VEGGIE NUGGETS
Serves 4

2 tablespoons extra-virgin olive oil

½ cup onion, chopped

1 garlic clove, minced

1 cup frozen mixed vegetables

½ cup water

1 cup cooked quinoa, any type

4 tablespoons nutritional yeast

½ cup breadcrumbs

2 tablespoons extra-virgin olive oil

There is nothing quite like the taste of a homemade vegan nugget, and the ease of knowing what ingredients you are using in them. These are delicious and nutritious, while also super easy to customize to use whatever ingredients you have on hand.

In a large frying pan or skillet on medium heat, sauté onion and garlic for about 3 minutes. Add mixed vegetables and stir frequently until very tender. Remove from heat and allow to cool enough to handle safely.

In a food processor, blend vegetable mixture and water and transfer to a large mixing bowl. Combine vegetable mixture, quinoa, and nutritional yeast. Roll into evenly sized balls (a scant 2 tablespoons per nugget works well) then press into ½ cup of breadcrumbs so the nugget is covered in breadcrumbs. The balls now change shape and become slightly flattened, oblong, oval, or whichever nugget shape you prefer.

In a large frying pan or skillet, sauté nuggets on medium heat in olive oil for 3–5 minutes each side, or until nuggets are crispy and cooked thoroughly. Serve with dipping sauces like ketchup, mustard, or barbeque sauce, if desired.

Tip: Don't have breadcrumbs? No problem! You can use crushed up crackers or put them in the food processor for a few pulses. You can also make your own breadcrumbs by processing bread in a blender or food processor until crumbly.

SPICY BUFFALO BAKED QUINOA NUGGETS

Serves 4

½ cup old-fashioned oats

½ cup water

1 tablespoon nutritional yeast

¼ teaspoon sea salt

½ cup cooked quinoa, any type

½ cup vegan butter, melted

⅛–¼ cup hot sauce or sriracha sauce

A lot of people enjoy the vegan buffalo nuggets or "wings" that are on the market, but wouldn't you prefer to have something a little less processed when you have the time to make them yourself at home? Yes, that's right—you *can* make them yourself at home and it is not as difficult as you might think!

Preheat oven to 400°F and line a large baking sheet with parchment paper or aluminum foil. In a food processor or blender, combine oats, water, nutritional yeast, and salt. In a large mixing bowl, fold cooked quinoa into oat mixture and form into evenly sized and shaped oval nuggets. Bake for 18–20 minutes or until slightly firm and crispy.

In a large mixing bowl, melted butter, and hot sauce together and toss nuggets in sauce. Return to baking sheet and bake for an additional 5 minutes. Serve with a cool dipping sauce, guacamole, plant-based sour cream, hummus, tomato ketchup, dressing, or anything you like.

Tip: You can change up the buffalo sauce mixture to make it more or less spicy. You can even change the flavor of these nuggets completely by making them teriyaki flavored or add a barbeque sauce flavor just by changing whatever sauce you toss them in.

PESTO QUINOA

WITH FRESH BASIL

Serves 4–6

¼ cup extra-virgin olive oil

¼ cup pine nuts

¼ cup fresh basil

2 cups cooked
   quinoa, any type

Salt and pepper, to taste

This is one of my go-to recipes that I like to make when I am craving something fresh *and* refreshing. This dish is a delight to make in the summer and makes a great appetizer, one that is more on the fancy side—perfect for cookouts.

In a blender or food processor, blend olive oil, pine nuts, and basil. In a large mixing bowl, toss cooked quinoa with pesto dressing and season with salt and pepper to taste. Serve immediately or refrigerate and serve chilled.

Tip: Double or triple this recipe and bring pesto quinoa to your next potluck or gathering. You will really impress with this simplistic yet mega-flavorful meal!

QUINOA TOPPED SWEET POTATOAST

Serves 2

1 tablespoon extra-virgin
    olive oil

2 large sweet potatoes

¼ cup cashew butter

½ cup cooked
    quinoa, any type

Salt and pepper, to taste

Sweet "potatoast" is easily one of my favorite meals to make, and with good reason. Sweet potatoes pack a real nutritional, punch with lots of fibers, vitamins, and minerals, and you may also be surprised to learn that they contain significant amounts of antioxidants. So topping sweet potatoes with a superstar food like quinoa really takes this meal to another level.

Preheat oven to 400°F and oil a large baking sheet with olive oil. Carefully slice each sweet potato lengthwise into four even slices. Place sweet potato slices on the baking sheet and flip over several times to coat each side lightly with olive oil. Bake for 20–25 minutes or until sweet potato slices are tender. Remove from oven and allow to cool slightly. Spread sweet potato slices with cashew butter and top with cooked quinoa. Season tops with salt and pepper to taste.

Tip: Experiment with using different nut or seed butters to spread on your sweet potatoast. You can even us hummus or vegan cheese spread. If you prefer a sweeter toast, use jam. Sweet pota-toast is a recipe you can get very creative with!

EASY QUINOA POUTINE

Serves 4–6

1 (25-ounce) bag frozen French fries, any type (shoestring is best for poutine)

2 cups vegan cheddar cheese, shredded

2 tablespoons vegan butter

½ cup all-purpose flour

4 cups vegan milk

¼ teaspoon sea salt

½ cup cooked quinoa, any type

2 tablespoons fresh parsley, chopped

Poutine was created in Canada in the 1950s and is used as a snack or light meal, combining pleasing flavors like cheese and gravy to top crispy French fries. Who wouldn't like that? Even better is this vegan version that adds healthy quinoa to the gravy. The quinoa also adds an interesting texture to the gravy which takes the place of curds in the traditional version of this dish. Poutine is a fun one to share during movie night. The only downside is that it is so yummy that before you know it, poof, poutine is all gone!

Bake the French fries according to package directions. Once cooked, turn off oven, top fries with cheddar cheese, then return to oven. This will allow the cheese to start to melt and keep the fries warm until you top with gravy, but since the oven is turned off, they will not be overcooked. In a medium saucepan on medium heat, melt butter and sprinkle in flour, stirring constantly. Gradually add in vegan milk and salt while whisking constantly. Reduce heat and cook, stirring continuously until gravy is thick and bubbly. Mix cooked quinoa into gravy and cook for a minute longer, or until quinoa is warmed thoroughly. Immediately top French fries with gravy and quinoa mixture to further melt the cheese. Garnish with parsley.

Tip: If you would like this poutine to be more authentic to the original recipe, try adding some baked tofu, as that could add even more texture to replace the curd in poutine. If you are pressed for time, consider using pre-made prepared gravy instead of making your own, which will make this poutine that much more of a breeze! If you want to make this recipe less processed, try making your own French fries instead of using store bought ones by air frying or baking potato slices.

PAN-FRIED QUINOA CAKES

Serves 4

½ cup canned chickpeas, drained and rinsed

⅛ cup water

¾ cup cooked quinoa, any type

2 tablespoons pimientos, chopped

½ teaspoon onion powder

¼ teaspoon garlic powder

1 tablespoon fresh parsley

¼ teaspoon sea salt

¼ cup breadcrumbs

2 tablespoons extra-virgin olive oil

I love the idea of vegan "crab" cakes but dislike that there is never any nutritional benefit to them when they are made the traditional way, with white flour and nearly no nutrient dense ingredients. These quinoa cakes will make you feel good about eating while enjoying this typical carnival or fair food!

In a blender or food processor, blend chickpeas and water and transfer to a large mixing bowl. Add cooked quinoa, pimientos, onion powder, garlic powder, parsley, and salt; mix well. Fold in breadcrumbs. Divide into eight balls then pat them down to form patty cakes. Set aside.

In a large frying pan or skillet on medium heat, sauté patties in olive oil until each side is golden, about 3–5 minutes per side.

Tip: These cakes can be topped with a dollop of your favorite vegan spread or can even be made into sandwiches or subs. Quinoa cakes taste amazing on top of salads.

CRANBERRY, KALE & QUINOA SALAD
Serves 4–6

2 cups cooked
    quinoa, any type

2 cups kale, stems removed

¾ cup dried cranberries

½ cup extra-virgin olive oil

¼ cup fresh lemon juice

2 tablespoons orange juice

¼ teaspoon garlic powder

Salt and pepper, to taste

Some recipes are so super simple to put together that at first glance they appear to be *too* easy—we assume they are bland, plain, or ordinary. That could not be further from the truth with vegan food. Quinoa in general has such a delicious, earthy, and nutty quality to it that when you add even the simplest ingredients, the dish just becomes dynamic. That is what this recipe is, in my opinion. It just seems way too easy to taste this spectacular.

In a large salad bowl, combine cooked quinoa, kale, and cranberries. In a small mixing bowl, combine olive oil, lemon juice, orange juice and garlic powder. Pour dressing over salad and toss. Season salad with salt and pepper, to taste.

Tip: Adding seasonal herbs to this salad is an extra-special addition. Pecans or walnuts can also be a nice treat. There are some lovely vegan feta cheeses out now, too, that would make great add-ons to this salad to switch it up sometimes, either for variety or curiosity's sake.

CHEESY QUINOA SQUARES
Serves 6–8

2 packages vegan filo or puff pastry

3 tablespoons vegan butter

2 tablespoons all-purpose flour

1 cup vegan milk

1 cup vegan cheese, shredded

2 tablespoons nutritional yeast

1 teaspoon onion powder

¼ teaspoon garlic powder

¼ teaspoon sea salt

3 cups cooked quinoa, any type

Ridiculously easy without having to prepare your own puff pastry, the cheesy sauce mixture melds so nicely with the quinoa. Once these cheese squares have settled, you have such a wonderful snack. These can be enjoyed warm or cold, either way they taste great!

Preheat an oven to 375°F and grease a 9 x 11-inch baking dish. Cover the bottom of the baking dish with one package's worth of puff pastry and bake for 12 minutes.

In a large saucepan on medium heat, melt vegan butter then whisk flour in slowly. Sauté for 2 minutes, then whisk milk in slowly. Warm milk, then add cheese, nutritional yeast, onion powder, garlic powder and sea salt. Stir frequently until sauce is bubbly and cheesy and cheese is melted. Stir in cooked quinoa and remove from heat. Pour the cheese quinoa mixture into the baking dish atop a bottom layer of puff pastry. Top with the last package of puff pastry, cover and bake for 40 minutes.

Cook uncovered for an additional 10–15 minutes or until top is golden. Remove and allow to set for 20 minutes. Cut into squares and serve.

Tip: These squares pair nicely with salad for a light lunch with flair.

AVOCADO QUINOA TOSS SALAD

WITH SPICY VINAIGRETTE

Serves 4–6

2 cups cooked
   quinoa, any type

3 cups mixed salad greens

2 ripe avocados, peeled
   and cubed

1 garlic clove, minced

¼ cup extra-virgin olive oil

¼ cup fresh lemon juice

2 tablespoons pure
   maple syrup

1 teaspoon sriracha sauce

½ teaspoon ground ginger

Salt and pepper, to taste

There is just something so special about avocado and quinoa together. Plus, adding salad greens and a spicy dressing that also lends a hint of sweetness is a nice change to the typical mundane salad we find ourselves getting too used to eating.

In a large salad bowl, combine quinoa, salad greens and avocado. In a small mixing bowl, combine garlic, olive oil, lemon juice, maple syrup, sriracha and ginger. Toss salad dressing in salad and season with salt and pepper, to taste.

Tip: Changing up the type of greens you use in this recipe each time you make it can be a real adventure. For a spicy and tangy treat, use arugula; for a more refreshing salad, try spring mixed greens; or, for a lighter salad, a combination of romaine and iceberg is particularly cool and fresh. Speaking of fresh: you can even add fresh herbs to your salad which gives out enormous flavor and is so interesting to boot.

TANGY THREE BEAN & QUINOA SALAD

Serves 6-8

1 cup canned kidney beans,
    drained and rinsed

1 cup canned cannellini
    beans, drained and rinsed

1 cup garbanzo beans,
    drained and rinsed

1½ cups cooked
    quinoa, any type

½ cup extra-virgin olive oil

¼ cup balsamic vinegar

2 tablespoons coconut sugar

1 garlic clove, minced

1 small onion,
    finely chopped

1 tablespoon fresh parsley

Salt and pepper, to taste

This delicious salad serves a crowd and keeps well in the refrigerator (in an airtight container) for about one week. It is fiber and protein rich and makes a great side dish on summer days and nights. Would be a great dish to bring to a cookout or when hosting outdoor gatherings this summer.

In a large salad bowl, combine all ingredients and toss together until well combined. Chill until ready to serve.

Tip: You do not have to only use the beans listed in this recipe. If you happen to have different canned beans on hand, it would be a welcome and tasty change to use them. Black beans also work well in this salad; experiment and try new things often!

QUINOA COATED GRAPES

Serves 10–12

1 tablespoon extra-virgin olive oil

¼ cup dry quinoa

1 cup vegan cream cheese

2 tablespoons powdered sugar

1 bunch grapes, washed

This appetizer is like the one that I remember my mom making when I was a child. My brother and I used to really love these grapes, so I decided to try it with quinoa as the coating instead of the typical chopped nuts. And what a pleasant surprise! It still reminded me of childhood, but I also got to incorporate one of my favorite new foods.

In a medium-sized saucepan on medium heat, heat olive oil and add quinoa. Stir quinoa frequently until all quinoa has popped. Remove quinoa from heat and allow to cool in a bowl. In a small mixing bowl, whip cream cheese and powdered sugar together. Roll each grape in the cream cheese mixture and roll in the popped quinoa to coat. Chill until ready to serve.

Tip: If you fancy something a little different, try adding sunflower, chia, or hemp seeds by replacing a few teaspoons to add to the popped quinoa. This will add to the beautiful visual appeal of the coated grapes while boosting its nutrition at the same time.

QUINOA TOPPED CHEESY GARLIC BREAD

Serves 8–10

1 large Italian bread loaf, sliced in half lengthwise

¼ cup vegan butter, softened

2 garlic cloves, minced

½ cup vegan parmesan cheese

1 cup cooked quinoa, any type

1 cup vegan mozzarella cheese, shredded

1 tablespoon extra-virgin olive oil

2 tablespoon fresh parsley, chopped

Salt and pepper, to taste

I got the idea for this recipe when I was on a cheesy garlic bread kick and was thinking about how carb heavy it was. I was wondering how I could possibly alter this recipe to make it more nutrient dense and add additional protein and fiber, when it occurred to me top with quinoa between the two layers of cheese! I had my doubts until I tried it, and now I'm so glad I can share this recipe with you. You will love it!

Preheat an oven to 350°F. Place loaf halves with middle side facing up on a large baking sheet. Spread the bread halves with vegan butter then sprinkle evenly with minced garlic and parmesan cheese. Top with cooked quinoa and cover with mozzarella cheese shreds. Drizzle with olive oil, sprinkle parsley and season with salt and pepper, to taste.

Tip: This garlic bread not only works well as a snack but can also be used as a side and served with pasta dishes. It would also go well on the side of a vegan "chicken" Caesar salad or even on the side with soups and stews.

QUINOA STUFFED GRAPE LEAVES

Serves 4–6

1 tablespoon vegan butter

1 small onion,
   finely chopped

1 garlic clove, minced

2 cups vegetable broth

1 cup dry quinoa

¼ teaspoon sea salt

¼ cup fresh dill, chopped

2 tablespoons fresh mint
   leaves, chopped

¼ cup fresh lemon juice

35 canned grape leaves,
   drained and rinsed

½ cup extra-virgin olive oil

Water

I have always loved stuffed grape leaves, but sometimes I feel that white rice leaves me feeling unsatisfied after consuming it. Then I tried making it using quinoa in the filling, and I may never go back. The unique texture of quinoa adds something so special to this classic dish and takes it up a notch.

In a large saucepan on medium heat, melt vegan butter and sauté onion and garlic. Deglaze the pan with vegetable broth and add uncooked quinoa; bring to a boil and reduce heat to a simmer. Cook quinoa until fluffy and water is absorbed, about 15–20 minutes, then remove from heat. Mix in salt, dill, mint, and lemon juice. Allow quinoa mixture to cool enough to safely handle.

Begin to stuff grape leaves with quinoa mixture by placing the shiny side of the grape leaf down and stuffing the opposite side. Stuff a scant teaspoon in each leaf, then fold each end of the grape leaves inward, and finally roll one end up and the other to close (like the way you would wrap a burrito).

Place rolled stuffed grape leaves in a large saucepan in rows, one on top of the other. Once all the grape leaves are stuffed, pour in olive oil and add water (just enough to cover them). Cook on low for 1 hour, allowing them to gently simmer but never boil. Remove from heat and allow to cool for 20 minutes, then use tongs to remove from liquid. Transfer to an airtight container, serving tray or platter.

Tip: Grape leaves will keep fresh in an airtight container in the refrigerator for up to one week.

EDAMAME QUINOA & FRESH HERB SALAD

Serves 4

1 cup cooked edamame

2 cups cooked
quinoa, any type

¼ cup fresh basil, chopped

2 tablespoons fresh
dill, chopped

2 tablespoons fresh
parsley, chopped

¼ cup extra-virgin olive oil

½ cup fresh lemon juice

Salt and pepper, to taste

Edamame quinoa and fresh herbs are among the world's most nutrient dense foods, and here they are all in one dish! Quite the surprise to see a salad so rich in healthy vitamins and minerals that is also super tasty. Or is it?

In a large salad bowl, toss all ingredients together until well combines. Chill until ready to serve.

Tip: If you ever run out of edamame, don't fret: sweet peas work great in this dish as well. Making substitutions that are similar to the ingredients you may not have on hand, or even ones that differ, often end up becoming the best dishes you will make.

HOMEMADE QUINOA CRACKERS

Serves 6-8

1 tablespoon extra-virgin olive oil

¼ cup dry quinoa

1 (15-oz) can chickpeas, drained and rinsed

½ cup old-fashioned oats

½ cup water

Salt and pepper, to taste

I have always loved making crackers at home. There's something about having freshly baked crackers on hand; it's such a treat. I used to make oat crackers and would sometimes add in nuts or seeds. I decided to try popped quinoa to my oat cracker recipe, and I'm so pleased that I did. These crackers are fiber-rich and so much healthier than the store bought kind. With just a few simple ingredients, you will have homemade crackers from scratch; how neat!

Preheat oven to 400°F and line a large baking sheet with parchment paper. In a medium saucepan on medium heat, heat olive oil and add quinoa. Stir quinoa frequently until all quinoa has popped. Remove quinoa from heat and transfer to a mixing bowl. In a blender or food processor, blend chickpeas, oats, and water; transfer this paste to mixing bowl and combine with quinoa.

Season dough with salt and pepper, to taste. Press dough evenly onto parchment paper on the baking sheet. Using a butter knife or spreader, gently carve out lines to where you will cut crackers off later. Bake for 10–12 minutes, or until crackers are firm enough to cut. Cut crackers and return to baking sheet; bake for 5 minutes longer. Allow crackers to cool.

Tip: These crackers will crisp up as they cool on the baking sheet, but they will crisp up even faster if you transfer crackers to a wire rack for cooling. These crackers are ideal for dipping or topping with your favorite spread. They can even be enjoyed as is, since they are delicious all by themselves.

QUINOA KALE CHIPS

Serves 4–6

1 bunch kale, stems removed

½ cup red bell
   pepper, chopped

¼ cup cashews

¼ cup nutritional yeast

¼ teaspoon sea salt

¾ cup water

½ cup cooked quinoa

Kale chips have been all the craze for a while now, and they are not going away any time soon! Another thing that has not been changing, though, is that kale chips are pricey. So why not make your own, and add quinoa to get a boost in your nutrients while you're at it? Homemade kale chips taste so much better and fresher, too!

Preheat an oven to 350°F and line a large baking sheet with parchment paper. Tear kale into smaller pieces and place in a large mixing bowl. In a blender or food processor, blend bell pepper, cashews, nutritional yeast, salt, and water; transfer to the mixing bowl. Add cooked quinoa to kale and mix all together until well combined and each piece of kale is well coated.

Transfer to baking sheet and spread evenly. Bake for 10–15 minutes or until kale chips are crispy but not burnt.

Tip: Almonds, as well as other nuts and seeds, work wonderfully in place of cashews in this recipe. If you do not have any cashews on hand, try using something else like sunflower seeds, or even pumpkin seeds.

SMOKEY QUINOA STUFFED POTATO SKINS

Serves 4

4 large russet potatoes

1 tablespoon extra-virgin olive oil

1 tablespoon vegan butter

½ onion, chopped

1 garlic clove, minced

¼ teaspoon sea salt

½ cup cooked quinoa, any type

4 tablespoons smoky or mesquite barbeque sauce

2 cups vegan cheddar cheese, shredded

Everyone loves potato skins…but what would you say if I told you that you can have them and have them be good for you? Well, here you have it: potato skins that are good for you! Potatoes are full of potassium and minerals and adding protein rich quinoa just adds to this super snack. This is also a high fiber recipe, so enjoy the wonderful health benefits while eating this classic comfort favorite.

Preheat an oven to 400°F and line a baking sheet with aluminum foil. With a fork, pierce several holes in the potatoes and rub with olive oil; bake for 45 minutes. Allow to cool enough to safely handle and cut potatoes in half.

In a large frying pan or skillet on medium heat, melt vegan butter and sauté onion and garlic then mix in salt and quinoa. Transfer to a large mixing bowl. Scoop out some of the middles of the potato halves and add to the mixing bowl; combine well. Scoop filling into potato skins, drizzle with barbeque sauce, and top with cheese shreds. Bake for 15 minutes longer, or until cheese has melted and tops have browned.

Tip: You can get creative with toppings with a recipe like this. Add green onion, dill, or even a drizzle of vegan ranch dressing right before serving. Your guests will be amazed.

LOADED QUINOA NACHOS

Serves 4–6

4 cups tortilla chips

2 tablespoons extra-virgin olive oil

½ cup onion, chopped

1 garlic clove, minced

1 cup cooked quinoa, any type

3 tablespoons taco seasoning

½ cup water

½ cup salsa

2 cups vegan cheddar cheese, shredded

½ cup guacamole

½ cup vegan sour cream

2 tablespoons green onion, chopped

This is exactly how I make my quinoa nachos, with the quinoa acting as the "veggie meat."

Preheat an oven to 350°F and line a large baking sheet with aluminum foil. Spread tortilla chips evenly on the baking sheet. In a large frying pan or skillet on medium heat, warm olive oil and sauté onions and garlic for 3–5 minutes. Add quinoa and taco seasoning and sauté, stirring constantly until quinoa starts to brown.

Deglaze pan with water and continue to cook until most of the water is absorbed. Spread quinoa evenly over tortilla chips then dollop salsa. Sprinkle vegan cheese shreds and bake for 15–20 minutes, or until cheese is melted and tortilla chips look lightly golden. Dollop guacamole and sour cream on top of nachos before serving. Garnish with green onion.

Tip: Play around with salsa types in this recipe! For example, if you want sweeter flavored nachos, use mango salsa. You can also use queso instead of cheese or in place of some of the cheese. You can really experiment with toppings and flavors in a recipe like this. Adding beans or a few dollops of refried beans also works nicely.

7-LAYER DIP

Serves 4–6

1 cup vegetable broth

½ cup dry quinoa

1 teaspoon taco seasoning

1 cup guacamole

1 cup salsa

1 cup vegan sour cream

1 cup vegan cheddar
  cheese, shredded

Before going vegan, I used a store bought layer dip. It was so delicious, and I wanted to recreate that type of taste and those flavors while using quinoa in place of the typical (and oftentimes fatty) refried bean layer. This 7-layer dip is awesome to serve up during your next get-together or to bring to a potluck with a bag of chips since everyone always loves it!

In a large saucepan on medium heat, bring broth to a boil. Add quinoa and taco seasoning, and reduce heat to a simmer. Cook until liquid is absorbed, about 15–20 minutes, then remove from heat and fluff quinoa with a fork. Set aside and allow to cool. In a trifle dish, serving bowl or container, layer first guacamole, then salsa, quinoa, sour cream, then sprinkle cheese shreds on top. Serve with tortilla chips or crackers.

Tip: In addition to serving this as a dip for chips or crackers, you can also serve this alongside tacos in order to skip having to put out bowls of each condiment, since most taco toppings are included in this dip. All it takes is a scoop of this dip on top of each taco and you only need a bowl for veggie "meat", shredded lettuce, beans, and whatever else you like to serve. This layer dip eliminates the need to have so many different bowls for condiments and lessens cleanup afterwards.

QUINOA FONDUE

Serves 6-8

2 tablespoons vegan butter

2 cups vegan milk,
   plain flavor

3 tablespoons
   nutritional yeast

1½ cups vegan cheese,
   any flavor

1 teaspoon onion powder

¼ teaspoon garlic powder

¼ teaspoon sea salt

⅛ teaspoon black pepper

¼ cup and 2 tablespoons
   cooked quinoa, any type

When I decided to add quinoa's unique texture to fondue, I did not expect to be so astounded. The quinoa doesn't just bump up the health value of this dish—it completely jazzes it up and takes it to a totally different level. When I dipped small slices of a French baguette into this amazing fondue, the creamy and cheesiness of the sauce itself, with the little bits of quinoa that complement but not overpower the dip...I was really blown away. Most of us would not really think to include superfoods like quinoa in dishes like fondues or dips. I think you will be happily surprised by this one, too.

In a large saucepan or fondue set on medium heat, melt vegan butter then whisk in vegan milk and nutritional yeast. Slowly stir in cheese and stir frequently until cheese is melted. Mix in onion powder, garlic powder, salt, and pepper. Fold in quinoa then heat thoroughly. Fondue is done when sauce is thickened.

Tip: We often think of dipping baguette bread slices in fondue, but keep in mind that there are other interesting choices to dip into fondue too. Try dipping raw or cooked veggies, baked tofu or vegan "meats", pita bread, crackers, chips, or pretzels.

RUSTIC QUINOA GRILLED CHEESE

Serves 2

¼ cup vegan butter

4 thick slices ciabatta bread

4 slices vegan cheese, any flavor

½ cup cooked quinoa, any type

I always love grilled cheese but it often leaves me feeling unsatisfied. Let's face it: grilled cheese is hardly a filling meal and I always end up serving it with a bowl of soup or stew and a dessert. Then it occurred to me to try it with quinoa in between two melty slices of vegan cheese and, oh boy, what a delight! I'll be making my grilled cheese this way as much as possible from now on!

Use half the butter to grease a large frying pan, skillet or griddle and heat to medium. Arrange grilled cheese sandwiches so that one slice of cheese is on each slice of bread and quinoa is in middle, two slices of cheese and ¼ cup of quinoa per sandwich. Spread the outsides of the grilled cheese sandwiches with remaining butter and grill for 3–5 minutes per side until crispy on the outside and melty inside.

Tip: This rustic grilled cheese goes splendidly with any soup or stew that you can imagine would be amazing with flaky ciabatta bread. I love pairing this grilled cheese with cabbage soups, vegetable soups or chunky stews.

TEA SANDWICHES

Serves 2

4 slices white bread

¼ cup vegan mayonnaise

½ cup cooked
    quinoa, any type

8 slices cucumber

2 tablespoons fresh dill

Salt and pepper, to taste

This is a twist on the classic tea or finger sandwich. As these usually include only cucumber as a main ingredient, they tend to be lacking in protein and don't quite fill you up. Adding quinoa to these types of sandwiches makes the meal a little more satisfying while still not too heavy, and still perfectly appropriate for your next tea party.

Cut the crusts off slices of bread and spread with mayonnaise. Press quinoa into the mayonnaise, then top each sandwich with cucumber slices and fresh dill. Before closing the sandwiches, season with salt and pepper, to taste. Cut each sandwich into four tea sandwich squares by cutting down the center vertically and diagonally.

Tip: To make these sandwiches lighter you can always replace the vegan mayonnaise with a light spread like hummus or a vegetable puree. You can also change flavors by replacing dill with another fresh herb like basil leaves.

GINGERY QUINOA "EGG" ROLLS

Serves 10

1 tablespoon extra-virgin olive oil

1 garlic clove, minced

1 tablespoon fresh ginger, minced

¼ cup cabbage, thinly sliced

½ cup cooked quinoa, any type

10 vegan eggroll wrappers

2 tablespoons vegan butter

Tip: If fresh ginger is unavailable to you, try using about ½ teaspoon of ground ginger instead.

Fun fact: vegan eggroll wrappers have become available on the market, and not just at specialty natural foods or health stores. Available at most grocery stores, these wrappers are so versatile and can be used for so many recipes, from savory to sweet. If you are lucky enough to get your hands on them, you can even store them in the freezer in batches and use as needed, since typically each package contains a lot of wrappers—more than you can use for one meal unless you are hosting a party.

In a large frying pan or skillet on medium heat, warm olive oil and garlic then add ginger and sauté for 1–2 minutes, then add cabbage and cook until the cabbage is tender. Mix in quinoa and cook a little longer until the quinoa is thoroughly warmed. Remove from heat and allow to cool enough to handle safely.

Place a small amount of quinoa filling in each eggroll wrapper and fold it like a small burrito by folding each side inward and rolling up and around. In a large frying pan or skillet on medium heat, melt butter and cook each eggroll for 3–5 minutes per side, or until outside is crispy and golden. Serve with your favorite dipping sauce.

ZUCCHINI NOODLE & QUINOA LASAGNA

Serves 6–8

2 large zucchinis, thinly sliced

1 cup cooked quinoa, any type

2 cups tomato sauce

¼ cup fresh basil, chopped

¼ cup fresh parsley, chopped

⅓ cup nutritional yeast

3 tablespoons extra-virgin olive oil

This is my go-to summertime lasagna. I just love lasagna casseroles, but in the summer, they can feel way too heavy. That is where this light and refreshing lasagna comes in. It does not bog you down, and the fresh herbs just make it taste ever so garden fresh. You will love serving this up for your family on those warm summer nights.

Preheat an oven to 350°F and grease a 9 x 11-inch baking dish. Layer casserole with zucchini slices, cooked quinoa, tomato sauce, sprinkles of fresh herbs, nutritional yeast, and drizzles of olive oil. Bake covered for 25 minutes and bake uncovered for an additional 15 minutes. Allow to cool slightly and set before cutting into 6–8 serving size squares.

Tip: Serve with a light bread or a side salad in the summer. If you would like to enjoy this dish during the cooler seasons, you can serve it with garlic bread or buttered, fresh ciabatta bread.

QUINOA SALSA

Serves 6–8

2 large tomatoes

1 small onion, peeled

1 garlic clove, peeled

1 tablespoon fresh cilantro

1 tablespoon fresh parsley

½ teaspoon sugar

2 tablespoons extra-virgin
   olive oil

1 tablespoon fresh lime juice

¼ cup water

¼ teaspoon sea salt

¼ teaspoon ground cumin

½ cup cooked
   quinoa, any type

Quinoa is one of the few grain-like ingredients that tastes awesome when chilled. Rice gets hard and does not always do well in salads for this reason; it certainly would not be able to compete against quinoa in this salsa. Quinoa works so well in this recipe as a salsa ingredient and boosts the nutritional value in it, all while taking nothing away from the freshness of this salsa.

In a blender or food processor, blend tomatoes, onion, garlic, cilantro, parsley, sugar, olive oil, lime juice, water, salt, and cumin. Transfer to a mixing bowl and fold in cooked quinoa. Chill salsa until ready to serve.

Tip: This salsa obviously pairs very well with chips, crackers, tacos and other dishes where salsa is called for, but consider using it in unexpected ways. Some creative uses for a fresh salsa like this would be atop a baked potato, or dolloped on casseroles to add a touch of freshness to heavier meals.

BAKED CAULIFLOWER "STEAKS"

WITH CHEESY QUINOA TOPPING

Serves 2–4

1 large head cauliflower

2 tablespoons extra-virgin olive oil

1 teaspoon onion powder

¼ teaspoon garlic powder

¼ teaspoon sea salt

⅛ teaspoon black pepper

⅛ teaspoon paprika

1 tablespoon vegan butter

1 cup vegan milk

¼ teaspoon nutritional yeast

1 tablespoon cornstarch

½ cup cooked quinoa, any type

I have been making cauliflower steaks this way for such a long time now, and while there is some protein content in cauliflower and other similar vegetables, adding a quinoa cheese sauce to this dish packs on even more protein and healthfulness.

Preheat an oven to 400°F and line a large baking sheet with aluminum foil. Wash cauliflower and remove the leaves and the thick part of stem. Cut the cauliflower into thick 1-inch slices. Rub olive oil on both sides of the cauliflower slices and place on baking sheet. Season with onion powder, garlic powder, salt, pepper, and paprika. Bake for 25–30 minutes or until cauliflower is tender and golden.

In a medium saucepan on medium heat, melt vegan butter, whisk in milk and warm. Whisk in nutritional yeast. In a small mixing bowl, carefully mix 2 tablespoons of the warm milk with cornstarch and return to saucepan. Whisk until bubbly and mix in quinoa; cook for 5 minutes, stirring frequently. Top cauliflower steaks with quinoa cheese sauce.

Tip: To increase the protein content of this recipe, you can use soy milk or any other high protein or protein-added vegan milk in the cheese sauce.

MINTY TOMATO GARLIC QUINOA OVER TOASTED PUMPERNICKEL BREAD

Serves 3–6

2 large ripe tomatoes, chopped

2 garlic cloves, minced

2 tablespoons fresh mint, chopped

1 tablespoon fresh basil, chopped

2 tablespoons extra-virgin olive oil

2 tablespoons fresh lemon juice

1 tablespoon pure maple syrup

½ teaspoon onion powder

¼ teaspoon sea salt

½ cup cooked quinoa, any type

6 slices pumpernickel bread

There is something so amazing about the flavor combination of fresh mint, tomato and pumpernickel. Adding in a superfood like quinoa was just a no-brainer. This recipe is very reminiscent of bruschetta but not so tiny in its portions. This is a hearty toast with generous portion sizes, so with quinoa as a perfect and complete protein and healthful ingredients like tomato and mint, this makes a wonderful light lunch.

In a large mixing bowl, combine tomatoes, garlic, mint, basil, olive oil, lemon juice, maple syrup, onion powder and salt. Fold in cooked quinoa and chill until ready to serve, then serve on toasted pumpernickel bread.

Tip: To make this a more filling lunch option or even a light spring or summer dinner choice, try pairing this dish with a nice soup. For an extra special treat, you can sometimes spread vegan butter or vegan cream cheese on the pumpernickel toast before topping with the quinoa mixture and serving. This dish makes an excellent late brunch option and pairs well with citrus-like fruit salads or citrus beverages.

QUINOA STUFFED ACORN SQUASH

WITH CASHEW RICOTTA

Serves 4

2 acorn squash, cut in half
    lengthwise

3 tablespoons extra-virgin
    olive oil

1 small onion,
    finely chopped

1 garlic clove, minced

2 cups cooked
    quinoa, any type

1 teaspoon Italian seasoning

½ cup cashews

1 tablespoon orange juice

2 tablespoons water

¼ teaspoon sea salt

A stuffed squash is such a cozy meal, but it's also on the lighter side. You get the best of both worlds with this recipe—the comforting taste of acorn squash with the light stuffing being mostly quinoa. If you would like to make this a heavier dish, you can add beans or tofu to the stuffing.

Preheat an oven to 400°F and place squash in a 9 x 11-inch baking dish, cut side up. In a large frying pan or skillet on medium heat, warm olive oil and sauté onions and garlic until aromas are released then add quinoa and Italian seasoning; sauté for 5 minutes, stirring often.

In a blender or food processor, blend cashews, orange juice, water, and salt. Stuff each acorn squash half with quinoa mixture and top with cashew ricotta. Bake uncovered for 35–40 minutes or until acorn squash is tender.

Tip: Use caution when cutting squash like acorn, which has a thick outer skin and a woody stem. Use a sharp knife or cut/peel the stem off before slicing in half, as this could make the work easier for you.

QUINOA STUFFED MUSHROOMS
Serves 4–6

2 teaspoons extra-virgin
  olive oil

20 white button mushroom
  caps, cleaned and
  stems reserved

2 tablespoons vegan butter

½ cup onions,
  finely chopped

2 garlic cloves, minced

¼ cup fresh basil, chopped

½ cup cooked
  quinoa, any type

Salt and pepper, to taste

Normally I like to stuff my mushrooms with bread-crumbs, rice, and even sometimes veggies or tofu, but in recreating this dish with quinoa, I've found I absolutely love it and cannot get enough. This is the type of meal that showcases quinoa as anything but boring.

Preheat oven to 375°F and line a large baking sheet with aluminum foil. Coat foil with olive oil and place the mushrooms cap side down and cavity side up. Chop mushroom stems, then in a large frying pan or skillet, melt vegan butter and sauté onions, garlic and chopped mushroom stems for 2–3 minutes. Add basil, quinoa, salt, and pepper.

Remove from heat and allow to cool just enough to safely handle. Stuff mushroom caps with filling. Bake for 15–20 minutes, or until mushrooms are tender.

Tip: Double or triple this recipe for when you are expecting company over. These stuffed mushrooms make for an excellent finger food for parties and get-togethers. It can also work well as a dish to take along to potlucks—just pack it in an airtight container.

LUNCH AND DINNER

✦

QUINOA MAKES A fantastic lunch or dinner option. A protein which contains nine essential amino acids and is rich in vitamins and minerals such as magnesium, iron, potassium, calcium, vitamins E and B, sufficient in beneficial antioxidants as well as high in fiber? That's definitely one to include in your main meals, lunch and dinner included. And since quinoa is so versatile, there are no limits to how you can prepare quinoa for these more filling meals.

QUINOA CRUST PIZZA

Serves 4–6

1 cup cooked
quinoa, any type

½ cup old-fashioned oats

½ cup vegetable broth

2 tablespoons extra-virgin
olive oil

3 tablespoons
sunflower seeds

1 teaspoon onion powder

¼ teaspoon garlic powder

¼ teaspoon sea salt

1 cup tomato sauce

1½ cups vegan
cheese, shredded

I love this pizza for several reasons, one of which is the absence of yeast. These days we tend to get an overload of yeast foods, so when there is an option to do a yeast-free crust, I like to take that route. With the presence of oats and quinoa, you are also getting gut-healthy fiber and an abundance of nutritional benefits all in the yummy meal that is pizza. What could be better than that?

Preheat an oven to 425°F and line a baking sheet with parchment paper. In a blender or food processor, blend cooked quinoa, oats, broth, 1 tablespoon of the olive oil, sunflower seeds, onion powder, garlic powder and salt. Form this dough mixture into a flat round crust on the parchment-lined baking sheet. Bake crust for 15–20 minutes. Remove crust from oven and top with tomato sauce, cheese, and remaining tablespoon of olive oil. Bake for 5 minutes longer, or until cheese is melted.

Tip: Change up your pizza style by adding different seeds to the crust or even by trying cashew nuts instead of sunflower seeds. Also, try using different types of sauces: you can use barbeque sauce, vegan "chicken" strips, and vegan cheddar cheese shreds for BBQ style pizza or add fresh herbs from your garden on top of your pizza for a burst of flavor.

MEATLESS CHILI WITH QUINOA

Serves 4–6

2 tablespoons extra-virgin olive oil

1 small onion, finely chopped

1 garlic clove, minced

1½ cups cooked quinoa, any type

1 (28-ounce) can crushed tomatoes

1½ cups water

1 (15-ounce) can kidney beans, drained and rinsed

2 tablespoons brown sugar

1 teaspoon ground cumin

1 teaspoon chili powder

1 teaspoon paprika

1 teaspoon dried basil

½ teaspoon dried oregano

Salt and pepper, to taste

You won't even miss the meat in chili after trying this one! This is a wonderful option to serve to those guests who kind of doubt whether vegan food can be tasty and are skeptical of quinoa but still curious enough to give things a try. This is the dish that will make them believers.

In a large saucepan on medium heat, sauté onions and garlic in olive oil until fragrant. Add quinoa to the pan and cook, stirring frequently, until lightly brown. Add remaining ingredients and simmer on low for about 25 minutes, or until flavors are well combined.

Tip: You can go spicier with this chili if desired; it is all up to your preference. You can add more chili powder if you want, I know I do! I like to just start with a mild chili that can appeal to everyone I am serving it to. You can also serve your chili with sriracha sauce on the side, so if someone wants to kick up the heat, they can do it on their serving, without making the entire dish spicy for everyone and those who may not prefer or tolerate spiciness very well.

GUMBO WITH QUINOA

Serves 6

½ cup extra-virgin olive oil

⅓ cup all-purpose flour

2 large onions, chopped

2 garlic cloves, minced

1 large green bell
pepper, chopped

1 (14-ounce) package vegan
sausages, chopped

2 cups tomatoes, chopped

¾ cup celery, chopped

1 (16-ounce) bag
frozen cut okra

2 quarts vegetable broth

1 cup water

1½ cups cooked
quinoa, any type

½ teaspoon ground
cayenne pepper

1½ teaspoon dried Italian
seasoning

Salt and pepper, to taste

Typically, I like gumbo with rice, but adding quinoa just makes sense to boost the protein and amino acid content. The flavor profile is amazing and adds a delightful nuttiness to the gumbo. The more firm texture of quinoa melds wonderfully with the mushier and more tender gumbo ingredients. Feel free to play around with the quinoa colors that you use; a deep red quinoa color will look beautiful with the green, brown and orange colors in the gumbo and really add to the visual appeal of your dish, especially so when serving to your guests.

In a large saucepan on medium heat, stir olive oil and flour together to make a roux. Keep stirring the olive oil and flour mixture until it begins toast and turn a golden brown color, then add onions, garlic, and pepper; roux will coat onions, garlic and pepper then cook until fragrant, stirring constantly.

Add to a saucepan chopped sausage, tomatoes, celery, okra, broth, water, cooked quinoa, cayenne pepper and Italian seasoning. Season with salt and pepper, to taste. Bring gumbo to a boil then reduce heat to low. Simmer for 20 minutes or until vegetables are tender.

Tip: You can control the spiciness by omitting the ground cayenne pepper for the gumbo to be less spicy or by adding more cayenne pepper to get more of that "heat."

GARLIC ONION QUINOA MINI CALZONES

Serves 6–8

16 ounces prepared
    pizza dough, divided
    into 6 pieces

3 tablespoons extra-virgin
    olive oil

2 garlic cloves, minced

¼ cup onion, finely chopped

¼ teaspoon dried basil

¼ teaspoon sea salt

1½ cups cooked
    quinoa, any type

½ cup tofu, cubed

1 cup vegan
    mozzarella cheese

1 tablespoon water

These calzones remind me so much of these little Italian baked breads that I used to enjoy from an Italian bakery. The quinoa in this recipe just takes calzones to another level. Feel free to enjoy these calzones as-is or by dipping them in your favorite marinara tomato sauce.

Preheat an oven to 425°F. On a lightly floured surface, roll out dough pieces into six flat rounds. Set aside on a parchment lined baking sheet.

In a large frying pan or skillet, sauté olive oil, garlic, onions, basil, and salt, until onion is tender. Add quinoa and stir fry for 3 minutes. Remove from heat and set aside.

In a blender or food processor, blend tofu, cheese, and water. Scoop stuffing mixture evenly into each dough round, top with a dollop of tofu cheese mixture, and fold dough in half to make calzones. Cut three small vents in the tops of calzones; this will allow steam to escape during baking, and bake for 15 minutes, or until dough is cooked completely and golden. Allow to cool for a few moments and for calzones to set before enjoying.

Tip: Play around with calzone fillings. You may want to add different flavor cheeses or different herbs and spices, too!

MANDARIN ORANGE ALMOND QUINOA ARUGULA WRAPS WITH SPICY DIPPING SAUCE

Serves 4

4 large sandwich
   tortilla wraps

½ cup canned mandarin
   orange segments, drained

¼ cup almonds, sliced
   or slivered

1 cup cooked
   quinoa, any type

2 cups arugula

½ cup vegan mayonnaise

1 tablespoon Dijon mustard

1 tablespoon pure
   maple syrup

1 teaspoon sriracha sauce

¼ teaspoon ground ginger

¼ teaspoon garlic powder

⅛ teaspoon sea salt

I used to get a delicious mandarin salad at a casino restaurant many years ago, but it had a lot of junk in it and no other greens beside iceberg lettuce. I liked the flavor and the idea of that salad, but I wanted something that tastes even better and was much more healthful. These wraps have healthy arugula, which you can swap for spinach or any other greens you have on hand, and almonds for a crunch factor. Making your own dipping sauce at home means you know exactly what ingredients are inside and the dressing always tastes way fresher this way.

In a large mixing bowl, combine mandarin oranges, almonds, cooked quinoa, and arugula; set aside. In a small mixing bowl, combine mayonnaise, mustard, maple syrup, sriracha sauce, ginger, garlic, and salt; transfer to four small bowls or ramekins for serving. Fill each wrap with quinoa and arugula mixture and roll up. Serve alongside dipping sauce.

Tip: To make these wraps warm, you can add vegan cheese inside of them, roll them up, and bake them in the oven until the outsides are toasty and the cheese is melted inside. They can also be sautéed in an oiled frying pan for a few moments on each side.

ONION, QUINOA AND "SAUSAGE" SAUTÉ

Serves 4–6

2 tablespoons extra-virgin
    olive oil

1 small onion, chopped

1 garlic clove, minced

4 large vegan
    sausages, chopped

1 cup cooked
    quinoa, any type

To make this recipe even quicker, grab cooked quinoa at the store. It is usually in the rice section next to the prepared rice in a foil bag type of packaging. Doing this (rather than always making your own) cuts down on time when you find yourself super busy.

In a large frying pan or skillet, sauté onions and garlic in olive oil on medium heat until fragrant. Add vegan sausage and cook until browned, then add the cooked quinoa. Sauté while stirring frequently until warmed, about 12 minutes.

Tip: Serve over greens to increase your vegetable intake, or serve with bread if you are already making a different vegetable side dish.

MESQUITE CHEESE TOPPED QUINOA BAKE

Serves 4–6

4 cups cooked
   quinoa, any type

1 cup vegan milk

2 cups vegan cheddar
   cheese, shredded

1 small onion, chopped

2 tablespoons pure
   maple syrup

1 teaspoon garlic powder

1 teaspoon paprika

1 teaspoon taco seasoning

¼ teaspoon cayenne pepper

⅛ teaspoon black pepper

There's just something about tangy mesquite flavors and vegan cheese that has them go together like best friends. Put them together in a bake and you have the perfect meal.

Preheat oven to 350°F and grease a 9 x 13-inch baking dish. In a large mixing bowl, combine cooked quinoa, milk, 1 cup of the cheese shreds, onion, maple syrup, garlic powder, paprika, taco seasoning, cayenne pepper and black pepper. Transfer to greased baking dish and top with remaining cheese shreds.

Bake covered for 30 minutes and uncovered for an additional 10–15 minutes or until casserole is bubbly and cheese is melted.

Tip: Control the spiciness or sweetness by adding more or less of those spices or ingredients like the syrup.

QUINOA BEET & "FETA" FLATBREAD

Serves 6

16 ounces prepared
pizza dough

½ cup tofu, crumbled

¼ cup vegan mayonnaise

¾ cup cooked
quinoa, any type

½ cup canned beets,
drained and sliced

2 tablespoons walnuts,
finely chopped

1 tablespoon extra-virgin
olive oil

Salt and pepper, to taste

You can never go wrong with a nice flatbread. Adding beets and quinoa together with your own homemade "feta" will make your taste buds happy. With simple ingredients making this meal is a breeze.

Preheat an oven to 450°F and grease a large baking sheet or pizza pan. On a lightly floured surface, roll out dough and arrange on pan. In a small mixing bowl, combine tofu and mayonnaise then spread evenly on dough. Spread on quinoa, beets, and walnuts atop pizza. Drizzle with olive oil and season with salt and pepper, to taste. Bake for 12–15 minutes or until dough is thoroughly cooked.

Tip: This flatbread pizza tastes scrumptious topped with whatever fresh herbs that you have on hand. If you grow your own herbs at home in your garden or on your windowsill indoors, adding some fresh dill, basil or thyme would taste really incredible

QUINOA LASAGNA

Serves 6–8

4 cups cooked
   quinoa, any type

3 cups tomato sauce

2 cups vegan
   beefless crumbles

2 cups vegan
   mozzarella cheese

¼ cup extra-virgin olive oil

This lasagna casserole is a bit different than the one we did earlier which uses zucchini slices as noodles. This lasagna uses cooked quinoa as the base of the lasagna and it really does make for a delicious, old timey casserole that you can scoop into your bowl and enjoy with a nice piece of buttered bread and cozy up with.

Preheat an oven to 350°F and grease a 9 x 11-inch baking dish. In a baking dish, layer cooked quinoa, tomato sauce, beefless crumbles, mozzarella cheese, and drizzles of olive oil, ending with the last layer being mozzarella on top drizzled with olive oil. Bake covered for 30 minutes, then uncovered for 10–15 minutes longer, or until cheese is melted and casserole is bubbly. Allow casserole to set and cool slightly before cutting into squares and scooping out to serve, using a serving spoon or large spatula.

Tip: This casserole can be used a sandwich or sub filling when you only have a little leftover and want to use it for lunch the next day. Just spread submarine, hoagie, or round sandwich rolls with vegan mayonnaise and add some fresh greens or sprouts to the sandwich, if you would like. Warm up the casserole and pat into the sandwich.

BAKED QUINOA CHEESY PARMESAN CASSEROLE

Serves 6–8

4 cups cooked quinoa,
   any flavor

1½ cups vegan milk

2 cups vegan cheddar
   cheese, shredded

1 teaspoon onion powder

½ teaspoon garlic powder

¼ cup vegan
   parmesan cheese

1½ cups breadcrumbs

¼ cup vegan butter, cut into
   small slices or cubes

If you are a fan of baked macaroni and cheese but get bogged down or even bloated after having too much wheat pasta, which a lot of us do, try this quinoa dish as a healthy alternative.

Preheat an oven to 375°F and grease a 9 x 11-inch baking dish. In a large mixing bowl, combine quinoa, milk, shredded cheese, onion powder and garlic powder, then transfer to the greased baking dish. Top casserole with parmesan cheese, then breadcrumbs. Evenly distribute pieces of butter atop of breadcrumbs; cover and bake for 25 minutes. Bake uncovered for 15 more minutes or until casserole is bubbly and golden on top.

Tip: This casserole is best served with a colorful side salad.

QUINOA FIESTA BOWL

Serves 2

1 cup cooked
   quinoa, any type

½ cup guacamole

½ cup roasted corn

½ cup salsa

½ cup vegan sour cream

24 tortilla chips

This recipe is so easy and comes together so quickly, especially if you cook a batch of quinoa ahead of time and keep it in the refrigerator in an airtight container for the couple of days that you are using it in recipes.

In a large mixing bowl, combine cooked quinoa, guacamole, roasted corn, salsa, and sour cream. Serve with tortilla chips.

Tip: Consider serving this over salad greens and crumbling up tortilla chips on top of a fiesta bowl.

QUINOA & SEAWEED SALAD

Serves 2

¼ cup dried wakame
seaweed, soaked
and chopped

2 cups mixed salad greens

10 grape or cherry
tomatoes, quartered

½ cup cooked
quinoa, any type

1 tablespoon fresh
lemon juice

1 tablespoon toasted
sesame oil

¼ teaspoon sea salt

1 teaspoon sesame seeds

The act of soaking seaweed is easy, but making seaweed salad often intimidates people. A lot of people have told me that they reserve seaweed salad for restaurants or buying pre-prepared at the grocery store. All you really need to do to make seaweed salad is soak seaweed (like wakame or nori) in warm water for a few moments and let it rehydrate. Most dried seaweed must rehydrate by soaking prior to eating. You can also add seaweed to soups and that will plump it right up too.

In a large salad or mixing bowl, toss seaweed, salad greens, tomatoes, quinoa, lemon juice, sesame oil and salt. Garnish with sesame seeds and serve.

Tip: All seaweeds are different, so whichever brand or type you choose, follow the package directions for rehydrating it.

QUINOA BAKED ZITI CASSEROLE

Serves 6–8

1 pound ziti pasta

1 (15-ounce) block firm tofu, drained

2 tablespoons extra-virgin olive oil

1 teaspoon dried Italian seasoning

2 tablespoons nutritional yeast

2 cups tomato marinara sauce

½ cup cooked quinoa, any type

I love the way the little pieces of quinoa look on the ziti in this pasta dish. This recipe makes for a lovely presentation and the quinoa gives some nice texture to the soft pasta, too.

Preheat an oven to 350°F and grease a 9 x 11-inch baking dish. In a large saucepan, cook ziti pasta according to package directions. In a blender or food processor, blend tofu, olive oil, Italian seasoning, and nutritional yeast. In a large mixing bowl, combine drained ziti pasta, tofu mixture, marinara sauce, and cooked quinoa. Transfer to a greased baking dish and bake covered for 30 minutes.

Tip: Play around with pasta sauces in this recipe. You can swap tomato sauce for a jar of creamy vegan alfredo sauce or use half tomato marinara and half alfredo. I have seen vegan alfredo and vodka sauces in the jarred sauce section of my local grocery stores by a popular pasta sauce maker, so I am sure you will be able to find that soon, too.

SWEET & PEPPERY ONION QUINOA SAUTÉ

Serves 4–6

3 tablespoons extra-virgin olive oil

1 large onion, sliced

2 garlic cloves, minced

1 tablespoon cane sugar

1 large bell pepper, julienned

1 cup cooked quinoa, any type

This recipe reminds me so much of peppery onion submarine sandwiches that used to be made at an Italian festival I would frequent while growing up, except it was usually being made with non-vegan meat like an animal sausage. But sometimes you would find that one vender that would make an all-vegetable version of this, to go right on a freshly baked hoagie roll. This is the quinoa version of that type of dish.

In a large frying pan or skillet on medium heat, warm olive oil and sauté onions and garlic for 1 minute. Sprinkle sugar on top and allow it to caramelize for about 45 seconds. Stir in bell pepper and stir fry until peppers are tender. Stir in quinoa and sauté until quinoa is warmed.

Tip: This sauté is awesome as is, used as filling in a hoagie roll or sandwich bun, or over salad greens. You can even add tomato marinara and cheese then broil to melt the cheese to add even more to this already awesome dish.

BUFFALO QUINOA

WITH COOL SOUR CREAM DILL DRIZZLE

Serves 4

2 cups cooked
   quinoa, any type

2 garlic cloves, sliced

¼ cup vegan butter melted

2 tablespoons hot sauce

½ cup cashews

¼ cup water

1 tablespoon extra-virgin
   olive oil

1 tablespoon fresh dill

¼ teaspoon sea salt

There is something just so phenomenal about a cool drizzled sauce with something spicy like this buffalo quinoa. It comes out fiery, sticky and the drizzle gives it that fresh "pop" you need in a dish like this.

Preheat an oven to 375°F and line a large baking sheet with aluminum foil and grease it. Evenly spread the cooked quinoa and garlic on baking sheet and drizzle with vegan butter and hot sauce. Bake for 20 minutes, stirring halfway through cooking. The quinoa is done when it is caramelized.

In a blender or food processor, blend cashews, water, olive oil, dill, and salt. Drizzle over buffalo quinoa and serve.

> **Tip:** This quinoa dish pairs awesome on top of salad greens and with fresh veggies with the drizzle making an excellent dressing. It also works very well in wraps or over pasta.

RATATOUILLE WITH QUINOA

Serves 6–8

3 tablespoons extra-virgin olive oil

7 garlic cloves, chopped

2 large onions, chopped

1 tablespoon cane sugar

¼ red wine

1 small green zucchini squash, peeled and cubed

5 small yellow squash zucchinis, peeled and cubed

1 large eggplant, peeled and cubed

1 small red sweet bell pepper, chopped

1 small yellow sweet bell pepper, chopped

1 (6-ounce) can tomato paste

2 cups water

1 cup cooked quinoa, any type

2 teaspoon dried parsley

1 teaspoon dried basil

½ teaspoon dried Italian seasoning

Salt and pepper, to taste

There are some foods that seems like they were just made for each other. All the ingredients in ratatouille are such a perfect match for quinoa, they go together magically. I think your taste buds will agree.

In a large stockpot, sauté garlic and onion in olive oil on low heat for 5 minutes, then stir in sugar and continue to caramelize on low heat, stirring occasional until garlic and onions are translucent. Deglaze pan with wine.

Add the remaining ingredients to the pan and mix thoroughly. Simmer on low heat for 1 hour, stirring occasionally until all vegetables are tender and fully cooked.

Tip: Serve with crusty French bread.

SHEPHERD'S PIE

Serves 6–8

2 tablespoons extra-virgin olive oil

1 large onion, chopped

1 garlic clove, minced

2 cups cooked quinoa, any type

2 tablespoons all-purpose flour

2½ cups vegetable broth

1 teaspoon dried Italian seasoning

½ cup frozen sweet corn

½ cup frozen green peas

1 teaspoon sea salt

4 large potatoes, peeled and cubed

¼ cup vegan butter

3 tablespoons vegan milk

This casserole is one of those wonderful dishes that can be thrown together quite easily but is still so darn impressive when you bring it out for guests or family members. I have never really met anyone so far who does not simply love shepherd's pie. The quinoa in this recipe replaces the "meat" that is typically used (or in my case, the vegan crumbles). I like using quinoa in shepherd's pie because it makes the whole dish feel unprocessed and it tastes much healthier.

Preheat oven to 375°F and grease a 9 x 13-inch baking dish. In a large saucepan on medium heat, sauté onions and garlic in olive oil until fragrant. Add cooked quinoa to pan and sauté, stirring frequently until lightly browned. Stir in flour, then slowly stir in broth and Italian seasoning; continue cooking while stirring frequently until sauce thickens slightly, then add corn and peas.

Sauté for about 5 minutes then transfer the mixture to a greased baking dish. Sprinkle half of the 1 teaspoon of sea salt on top of the vegetable quinoa mixture. Add cubed potatoes to a large saucepan and add water to the pan, just enough to cover potatoes. Bring to a boil and simmer on medium for about 20 minutes or until potatoes are tender. Drain potatoes and add back to the empty saucepan with vegan butter, milk, and the other half of the salt. Mash until well combined, then spread evenly on top of vegetable mixture in baking dish. Bake uncovered for 35–40 minutes. Let casserole sit for about 10 minutes or so to set before serving.

Tip: Instead of a half cup of sweet corn and a half cup of green peas, you can use 1 cup of frozen mixed vegetables in this recipe.

QUINOA STUFFED PEPPERS

Serves 4

4 large bell peppers,
any color

2 tablespoons extra-virgin
olive oil

1 large onion, chopped

1 garlic clove, minced

1 cup cooked
quinoa, any type

1 teaspoon dried Italian
seasoning

3 tablespoons vegan
parmesan cheese

2 cups vegan mozzarella
cheese, shredded

2 cups tomato
marinara sauce

Salt and pepper, to taste

I remember fondly the days as a child when everyone would gather around the table once the stuffed peppers were ready. Growing up, they were such a special treat that we all loved and enjoyed. To this day, I still make stuffed peppers and think of those fond memories. Food really brings family together and adds joy to your heart. Making these stuffed peppers with quinoa instead of rice has done nothing to change how comforting and enjoyable this recipe is.

Preheat oven to 350°F and grease a square baking dish. Cut across the top of each bell pepper, removing the stem and seeds. Place peppers in a greased baking dish.

In a large frying pan or skillet on medium heat, sauté onions and garlic in 1 tablespoon of the olive oil until fragrant. Add cooked quinoa and sauté until lightly browned. Remove from heat and mix in Italian seasoning, parmesan cheese, 1 cup of the mozzarella cheese shreds, and 1 cup of the marinara sauce. Season with salt and pepper, to taste.

Spoon this filling into each pepper and push down gently to fill them all evenly. Top peppers with the remaining marinara sauce and cheese shreds. Drizzle with the remaining tablespoon of olive oil. Bake covered for 30 minutes, then bake for an additional 10–15 minutes uncovered, or until bell peppers are tender and cheese on top is melted.

Tip: For a change in flavor, you can use different sauces instead of the typical tomato marinara sauce. You can even use salsa for more Southwestern flavored stuffed peppers.

QUINOA CURRY

Serves 4–6

¼ cup vegan butter

1 large onion, chopped

1 large green bell pepper, chopped

1½ cup cooked quinoa, any type

1 tablespoon all-purpose flour

½ tablespoon curry powder

1 teaspoon sea salt

¼ cup water

⅛ cup fresh lemon juice

1 cup tomato marinara sauce

1 garlic clove, minced

You might not always think of pairing curry with quinoa, since curries are typically served with rice or even naan, but by adding quinoa to this dish in place of tofu or a veggie "meat", you get a curry with an amazingly unique flavor and texture.

In a large saucepan on medium heat, melt butter and sauté onion and bell pepper until tender. Add quinoa and stir fry until lightly browned. Stir in flour, curry powder, and salt, then slowly stir in water. Continue to stir until the curry reaches a paste consistency.

Add tomato sauce and garlic; reduce heat to simmer. Simmer on low heat for 20 minutes, stirring occasionally.

Tip: You can enjoy this as is, served with naan, or enjoy it over a rice like basmati.

SPICED QUINOA BOWL

Serves 4–6

2 cups vegetable broth

1 cup dry quinoa, any type

½ cup broccoli, chopped

½ cup onion, chopped

1 garlic clove, minced

1 dried bay leaf

1 teaspoon ground turmeric

½ teaspoon ground cumin

¼ teaspoon ground ginger

This spiced quinoa bowl is wonderful just like this, but does even better topped with baked tofu or another vegan protein.

In a large saucepan on medium heat, combine all ingredients and bring to a boil. Reduce to simmer and cover; simmer for 20 minutes or until liquid is reduced and quinoa is fluffy. Fluff quinoa with fork and remove bay leaf prior to serving.

Tip: Change up the spices according to what you have on hand in your pantry or what flavors you are in the mood for. You can even use taco seasoning in this dish, which tastes great, too!

SIDE DISHES

★

HAVE ALWAYS CONSIDERED side dishes to be the underappreciated stars of the show—a big part of the meal and one that is truly important. A meal can be going all wrong…until you bring out just the right side to tie it all together and make it spectacular. Maybe you're entertaining and need a couple of side dishes to add to the meal—it's the simple additions that make it perfect. Or maybe you are looking for one small thing that is super easy and fast to prepare but will totally takes your mealtime to another level. Side dishes save the day. This section is about lightning fast quinoa recipes that can be prepared without thinking twice, but really help to turn a bunch of dishes into a real meal.

QUINOA & CHEESE SIDE

Serves 6–8

2 tablespoons vegan butter

½ onion, finely chopped

1 cup vegetable broth

1 cup vegan milk

1 cup dry quinoa, any type

2 cups vegan cheese,
  any flavor

Salt and pepper, to taste

A scoop or two of this dish alongside your meal *really* makes it special. Whether you serve this at home alongside your lunch or dinner (or perhaps even brunch), or bring a big casserole to the next potluck that you are invited to, this cheesy quinoa classic is sure to please.

In a large saucepan on medium heat, melt vegan butter and sauté onion for a few moments. Add broth, milk, quinoa, and cheese to the saucepan and stir until well combined. Cook on low heat until liquid is mostly reduced, stirring occasionally. Season with salt and pepper, to taste.

Tip: This side should resemble risotto, but using quinoa instead of rice. One way to know when the dish is done is to try a little bit of it yourself; the quinoa should be fluffy and well done, but also have just a touch of firmness to it as well.

FLUFFY QUINOA WITH FRESH BASIL SAUCE

Serves 4–6

2 cups vegetable broth

1 cup dry quinoa, any type

2 teaspoons dried Italian seasoning

¼ cup fresh basil

2 tablespoons extra-virgin olive oil

Salt and pepper, to taste

This is the perfect side dish to accompany the many delicious Italian dishes available. With a seriously fresh taste all its own, this is delightful to enjoy in the warmer summer months. It is also a great one to serve alongside grilled barbeque food during a cookout: the freshness adds a bit of contrast to those heavy, bready, and smoky BBQ foods.

In a large saucepan on medium heat, bring vegetable broth to a boil. Add quinoa and Italian seasoning and simmer on low heat until liquid is reduced and quinoa is fluffy. Fluff with a fork.

In a blender or food processor, blend basil, olive oil and salt and pepper, to taste. Drizzle basil sauce over fluffy quinoa.

Tip: To make this an even more substantial side dish, consider serving over salad greens and top with chopped, fresh vegetables like tomato, zucchini, or whatever combinations you can imagine.

ELEGANT CREAMY QUINOA SALAD STUFFED AVOCADO

Serves 2–4

2 large ripe avocados

¼ cup cooked
   quinoa, any type

¼ cup vegan mayonnaise

¼ cup tomatoes, chopped

½ teaspoon onion powder

Salt and pepper, to taste

This is such a pretty, classy-looking yet petite stuffed salad. Use this recipe for elegant lunch dates where you are the host of the afternoon; I bet your guests will just rave about this dish! For more visual appeal, garnish with a sprig of dill or a mint leaf.

Wash avocados and cut them in half lengthwise. Remove avocado pits and discard. Carefully scoop out avocado flesh, being careful to keep avocado shells intact. Set shells aside.

In a mixing bowl, combine avocado flesh, cooked quinoa, vegan mayonnaise, tomatoes, onion powder. Season with salt and pepper to taste. Transfer mixture back into avocado halves.

Tip: Do *not* eat the avocado skins; they just act as "bowls" for a pretty presentation.

QUINOA ALFREDO BALLS

Serves 10

2 cups cooked
   quinoa, any type

1 (8-ounce) container vegan
   cream cheese, softened

1 teaspoon onion powder

½ teaspoon garlic powder

½ teaspoon sea salt

1 cup breadcrumbs

Part arancino and part something else entirely and uniquely its own, these are ridiculously easy to put together! Serving this side dish alongside your pasta, soups or salads is such a breeze, yet so fancy and impressive.

Once cooked, allow quinoa to cool enough to safely handle. In a large mixing bowl, combine cream cheese, onion powder, garlic powder and salt. Form into ten balls and roll into breadcrumbs.

   Air fry at 400°F for 10 minutes. Alternatively, you can you pan fry in vegan butter or vegetable oil for 10 minutes, turning the balls to cook each side after several minutes.

Tip: This quinoa alfredo can be served with tomato marinara sauce for dipping, or even barbeque sauce.

WALNUT GRAPE QUINOA ON CROSTINI
Serves 6–8

1 French baguette, sliced

¼ cup vegan butter, melted

½ cup walnuts chopped

½ cup grapes, quartered

¼ cup cooked
    quinoa, any type

2 tablespoons fresh
    orange juice

1 teaspoon balsamic vinegar

1 teaspoon pure maple syrup

1 tablespoon extra-virgin
    olive oil

⅛ teaspoon sea salt

⅛ teaspoon black pepper

I love anything on crostini. What a fantastic side dish to serve with just about any meal, but I especially love this recipe alongside a nice soup. When I serve comfort foods, I love to also have a pop of something fresh tasting or refreshing. This side dish is a fun twist on a tapa.

Preheat oven to 350°F. Arrange baguette slices on two large baking sheets. Brush both sides with melted butter and bake for 15 minutes or until crispy and toasted.

In a large mixing bowl, combine walnuts, grapes, cooked quinoa, orange juice, vinegar, maple syrup, olive oil, salt, and pepper. To assemble crostini, use mixture top toasted baguette slices.

Tip: If you find yourself running out of walnuts, almonds also taste splendid in this crostini recipe!

SWEET & SOUR QUINOA SAUTÉ

Serves 4–6

1 tablespoon extra-virgin olive oil

1½ cups cooked quinoa, any type

1 cup kale, thinly sliced

¼ cup sweet and sour sauce

This side dish has so much in common with sweet and sour "chicken" (except for the cruelty and unhealthiness, of course). Pair this side with spicy noodles, ramen, pho, or alongside your next stir fry.

In a large saucepan or skillet, warm olive oil and sauté cooked quinoa until lightly brown. Add kale and sauce; sauté until kale is cooked and quinoa is heated thoroughly.

Tip: This side dish is versatile and can also be served with any style cuisine. It can be eaten alongside sandwiches for lunch or with a vegan roast for dinner; it's the ideal side dish for when you need a little something more to go with a meal, and really want to wow the people you are cooking for.

QUINOA PEAR ARUGULA & HERB SALAD **WITH SPARKLING CIDER VINAIGRETTE**

Serves 4

3 cups arugula

1 cup cooked quinoa, any type

1 pear, peeled and thinly sliced

2 tablespoons fresh dill, chopped

1 tablespoon fresh mint leaves, chopped

1 tablespoon fresh basil, chopped

¼ cup sparkling cider

2 tablespoons balsamic vinegar

1 tablespoon extra-virgin olive oil

Salt and pepper, to taste

For some reason, quinoa works well in even the most sophisticated salads. That is why I knew this protein-packed seed would be incredible in a pear, arugula, and fresh herbs combo, especially one that is tossed in a light and beautiful sparkly vinaigrette. It's almost too pretty to eat!

In a large salad bowl or mixing bowl, toss arugula, quinoa, pear, dill, mint, and basil. In a small mixing bowl, whisk together cider, vinegar, olive oil. Season with salt and pepper, to taste. Dress salad with vinaigrette and chill until ready to serve.

> **Tip:** You can swap the arugula for any other salad greens. Baby spinach works nicely, as do mixed salad greens and various styles of romaine.

TERIYAKI QUINOA STIR FRY SIDE

Serves 4

3 tablespoons vegan butter

½ cup onion, chopped

1 tablespoon fresh ginger, minced

2 cups cooked quinoa, any type

¼ cup teriyaki sauce

This is the perfect side to go with a nice noodle soup or a delicious tofu dish if you want something other than rice or bread to go along with it. Earthy ginger adds strong but pleasing flavors to this mouthwatering side dish.

In a large frying pan or skillet on medium heat, melt vegan butter and sauté onion and ginger for 3–5 minutes. Add quinoa and teriyaki sauce and stir fry until well combined and thoroughly warmed.

Tip: To make this side dish a little more healthful, add broccoli and thinly sliced carrots during the sautéing process.

QUINOA GRAPEFRUIT BRUNCH-STYLE SIDE

Serves 4–6

2 large grapefruits, peeled and sectioned

2 cups cooked quinoa, any type

1 tablespoon extra-virgin olive oil

2 tablespoons fresh orange juice

1 tablespoon pure maple syrup

2 tablespoons fresh mint leaves

¼ teaspoon ground nutmeg

Sea salt to taste

When I think of grapefruit, I think of the beginning of spring and summer time, the sunny weather, and eating less of those heavy comfort foods, instead enjoying more refreshing and lighter fare. This side dish works well all year round but is especially fitting in the warmer weather months.

In a large salad bowl or mixing bowl, toss grapefruit, cooked quinoa, olive oil, orange juice, maple syrup, mint leaves, and nutmeg. Season with salt to taste.

Tip: This can be served as-is in beautiful serving cups, champagne glasses or decorative ramekins, or it can also be served over a bed of mixed salad greens.

MUSTARD SAUERKRAUT QUINOA PICNIC-STYLE SIDE

Serves 4–6

1 (15-ounce) can
   sauerkraut, drained

½ cup cooked
   quinoa, any type

2 tablespoons Dijon mustard

1 tablespoon pure
   maple syrup

¼ cup carrots, shredded

I love that crunchiness of crisp and cold sauerkraut, but oftentimes it is too sour to enjoy a heaping spoonful, so I wanted to make something similar to sauerkraut and also incorporate quinoa. This side dish is amazing on a warm, sunny day.

In a large salad bowl or mixing bowl, combine all ingredients. Chill until ready to serve.

Tip: This side dish is best served chilled and cold. It is the perfect picnic or cookout food, and can also be used to top veggie hotdogs or veggie burgers.

QUINOA SALAD STUFFED TOMATOES

WITH AVOCADO TAHINI DRESSING

Serves 2

½ cup cooked
    quinoa, any type

½ cup vegan mayonnaise

2 large tomatoes,
    scooped out

1 teaspoon Dijon mustard

1 teaspoon cane sugar

1 ripe avocado

2 tablespoons tahini

1 tablespoon water

¼ teaspoon sea salt

These adorable and delectable stuffed tomatoes are so extraordinarily easy! They only appear complicated. This should be a go-to for when you want your family to be super impressed and to think you have been working extra hard in the kitchen, even though this side dish comes together in mere minutes.

In a mixing bowl, combine cooked quinoa, vegan mayonnaise, mustard, and sugar with tomato filling. Use filling to stuff tomato in the empty space where you scooped out the middles.

In a blender or food processor, blend avocado, tahini, water, and sea salt. Drizzle on top of stuffed tomatoes.

Tip: If you want to increase the wow factor of a simple lunch like a sandwich, especially a grilled cheese sandwich, serve it with these stuffed tomatoes.

TUTTI FRUITY QUINOA SIDE

WITH HOMEMADE WHIPPED TOPPING

Serves 4

1 cup cooked
  quinoa, any type

½ cup mandarin
  orange segments

½ cup fresh blueberries

¼ cup dried cranberries

1 tablespoon pure
  maple syrup

2 tablespoons fresh
  orange juice

1 cup vegan heavy
  whipping cream

¼ cup powdered sugar

⅛ cup walnuts, chopped

It is not very often you get to combine fruits with a perfect protein like quinoa. There just are not very many opportunities to do something as nutritional packed as this…until this recipe came along, that is!

In a large serving bowl, combine quinoa, mandarin oranges, blueberries, cranberries, maple syrup and orange juice. Chill until ready to serve.

When ready to serve, combine whipping cream and powdered sugar and whip until stiff peaks are formed (using a hand mixer or stand mixer is best, although you can whisk by hand—it will just take longer). Dollop whipped topping on side dish and garnish with chopped walnuts.

Tip: Vegan heavy whipping cream is now available by the popular vegan milk brands and located in your local grocery store's refrigerated non-dairy milk section.

QUINOA TOFU GRAVY SAUCE OVER HOMEMADE BISCUITS

Serves 8–10

GRAVY

¼ cup vegan butter

½ cup tofu, crumbled

¼ cup cooked
    quinoa, any type

½ cup all-purpose flour

4 cups vegan milk

¼ teaspoon sea salt

BISCUITS

2 cups all-purpose flour

1 tablespoon baking powder

½ teaspoon salt

½ cup extra-virgin olive oil

½ cup vegan milk

Cozy biscuits and gravy are such a classic side dish that I am overjoyed that I was able to create this amazing gravy using tofu and quinoa in place of the "meat" that is typically used in a gravy like this. You will be delighted with the texture and flavors in this side dish.

In a large saucepan on medium heat, melt vegan butter and sauté tofu and quinoa until browned. Sprinkle flour over the mixture then slowly stir in milk and salt. Stir continuously until gravy is thick and buttery.

Preheat oven to 450°F and very lightly grease a large baking sheet. In a large mixing bowl, combine flour, baking powder and salt. Combine olive oil with milk and slowly add to dry mixture. Mix thoroughly and gently knead dough. On a lightly floured surface, roll out dough and cut out 10 circles, ½ inch in thickness, using a biscuit cutter. Bake for 10 minutes or until biscuits are lightly brown, have risen and appear fluffy.

Tip: You are going to end up making this recipe a lot, I'm guessing, so for variety's sake, you can change up the flavors of the gravy or biscuits. Rosemary and thyme are scrumptious fresh herbs to add to the gravy or even the biscuits, or you could consider adding vegan cheese to your biscuits to jazz things up.

MINI QUINOA EASTER PIES

Serves 12

2 cups all-purpose flour

¼ cup vegan butter

½ cup water

1 cup firm tofu, drained and cubed

¼ cup vegan milk

½ cup cooked quinoa, any type

1 teaspoon onion powder

½ teaspoon garlic powder

½ teaspoon sea salt

1 cup vegan cheese, shredded

Pizzagaina is my inspiration for these mini Easter pies. *Pizzagaina* is an Italian ham pie traditionally served at Easter time, and I wanted to take that concept and replace a lot of the processed ingredients with healthful quinoa and tofu. Here is what I came up with.

Preheat oven to 400°F and line a muffin pan with 12 liners. In a large mixing bowl, combine flour, butter, and water to make a dough. On a lightly floured surface, gently knead dough and roll out. Divide into 12 pieces, form into balls and flatten into each muffin liner.

In a blender or food processor, blend tofu and milk; transfer to a large mixing bowl. Add to mixing bowl the cooked quinoa, onion powder, garlic powder, salt, and shredded cheese. Scoop mixture into each muffin liner, atop dough crust. Bake for 20 minutes or until dough crust is cooked thoroughly. Allow mini pies to cool slightly and set before enjoying.

Tip: These mini pies can be enjoyed cold or warm. They are traditionally enjoyed warm once baked, cold the following day, and sometimes reheated for when you want to enjoy them melty again.

COCONUT GINGER QUINOA SIDE

Serves 4–6

2 cups cooked
   quinoa, any type

1 tablespoon fresh
   ginger, minced

1 cup coconut, shredded

1 tablespoon coconut
   oil, melted

Salt and pepper, to taste

This is an awesome side dish on its own *and* as a salad topper.

Preheat oven to 400°F and grease a large baking sheet. Spread quinoa, ginger, and coconut on baking sheet. Drizzle with melted coconut oil. Season with salt and pepper, to taste. Bake for 20 minutes.

> **Tip:** Try adding nuts like pecans or almonds to baking sheet for a variation in flavors and texture.

DESSERTS

Possibly the most unexpected section of any quinoa cookbook— the dessert chapter! Yes, quinoa is one of those multitaskers that can be ground up and used as flour in baking, but I'll bet you didn't know it can also be toasted or popped and included in candy bars and other sweet treats.

QUINOA & OATMEAL COOKIES

Serves 10–12

1 tablespoon extra-virgin olive oil

¼ cup dry quinoa

2 cups all-purpose flour

1 cup old-fashioned oats

1 teaspoon baking soda

¼ teaspoon sea salt

1 cup coconut oil, melted

½ cup brown sugar

¼ cup warm water

½ teaspoon pure vanilla extract

These are not your grandma's oatmeal cookies. These are trendy quinoa oatmeal cookies and are worthy of a social media photograph post with all the filters and hashtags.

Preheat oven to 350°F and line a large baking sheet with parchment paper. In a medium-sized saucepan on medium heat, heat olive oil and add quinoa. Stir quinoa frequently until all quinoa has popped. Remove quinoa from heat and add to a large mixing bowl.

In the mixing bowl with the quinoa, add flour, oats, baking soda, salt. In another large mixing bowl, combine wet ingredients, coconut oil, brown sugar, warm water and vanilla and stir until brown sugar is dissolved. Add wet and dry ingredients together and roll cookies into 24 balls and slightly press down to flatten on baking sheet. Bake for 10–12 minutes and allow cookies to cool slightly and firm up some.

Tip: These cookies store well at room temperature in an airtight container, but I always like to store mine in the refrigerator (again in an airtight container) for maximum freshness and to make them last longer. The cookies will keep for about one week, though you can always freeze them in freezer bags for up to one month. When ready to use, just defrost and they will be as soft as they were when you first made them.

CHOCOLATE CHIP QUINOA COOKIES

Makes about 2 dozen cookies

1 tablespoon coconut oil

¼ cup dry quinoa

2 cups all-purpose flour

1 cup mini vegan
   chocolate chips

1 teaspoon baking soda

¼ teaspoon sea salt

½ cup vegan butter, melted

1 cup brown sugar

½ cup vegan milk

These chocolate chip cookies made with popped quinoa are melt-in-your-mouth good. You will love them!

Preheat oven to 375°F and line two large baking sheets with parchment paper. In a medium-sized saucepan on medium heat, heat coconut oil and add quinoa. Stir quinoa frequently until all quinoa has popped and transfer to a bowl to cool.

Once cooled, add flour, chocolate chips, baking soda and salt. Melt butter and brown sugar together and when sugar is dissolved, add milk and combine with dry ingredients. Roll dough into balls and place on baking sheets about 1 inch apart. Bake for 10–12 minutes and allow to slightly cool and set.

Tip: If vegan mini chocolate chips are not available, you can also use a chocolate bar and chop it into small chunks.

QUINOA PUDDING

Serves 4

6 cups vegan milk, divided

½ cup cane sugar

2 teaspoons pure
vanilla extract

½ teaspoon sea salt

½ cup golden raisins

¼ cup almonds, slivered

½ cup dry quinoa

½ cup white rice

¼ teaspoon
ground cinnamon

⅛ teaspoon ground nutmeg

There's a particular rice pudding that I often get from a restaurant and I wanted to try and recreate those flavors while incorporating quinoa in some way while adding my own personal touches. Particularly, I wanted to cross the flavors and textures of old-fashioned rice pudding with the Thai pudding that I really like. I also wanted to include a little rice, too, because that lends to the starchiness we desire in the consistency and result of the dish.

In a large saucepan, bring 5 cups of the milk to a gentle boil, then add sugar, vanilla, salt, raisins, almonds, dry quinoa and rice. Reduce heat and allow to gently simmer for about 1 hour, stirring occasionally. The pudding will be ready when it reaches a thick and creamy consistency. Remove from heat and stir in remaining cup of milk, cinnamon, and nutmeg. Allow to cool, then refrigerate.

Tip: The ratio of milk to quinoa and rice might look a little odd, but never fear: it will reduce and become creamy goodness, it just takes some time. This pudding is best enjoyed super cold, so chill in the refrigerator for several hours (chilling overnight is best).

CRISPY QUINOA TREAT SQUARES

Makes 2 dozen squares

6 cups popped or puffed quinoa

4 tablespoons vegan butter

1 (10-ounce) package vegan marshmallows

Do you remember those fluffy marshmallow and crispy cereal treats you enjoyed as a kid? I do! Before vegan marshmallows were available, we had to make our own marshmallows for this one. However, with the invention of vegan-friendly marshmallows and the abundance of their availability at so many different supermarkets now, it is easy to make these treats while still following a plant-based diet. I wanted to try them with popped quinoa instead of puffed rice cereal, and they turned out just as amazing as I thought they would. The added protein really helps me feel better about eating way too many of these treats!

Grease a 9 x 13-inch baking dish. In an extra-large mixing bowl, place popped or puffed quinoa. In a small saucepan, melt butter and vegan marshmallows and mix into puffed quinoa. Press quinoa into greased baking dish and allow to set in refrigerator for 2 hours then cut into squares.

Tip: These can be made using puffed quinoa as well, though that's not as readily available as dry quinoa you pop on your own. Puffed quinoa is much bigger in size and resembles puffed rice cereal.

QUINOA BROWNIES

Makes 1 dozen brownies

1 tablespoon coconut oil

¼ cup dry quinoa

2 cups all-purpose flour

1 cup powdered sugar

¾ teaspoon sea salt

¾ cup cocoa powder

1 teaspoon baking powder

1 cup warm water

1 cup brown sugar

¼ cup pure maple syrup

1 teaspoon pure
   vanilla extract

½ cup vegan butter, melted

1 cup chocolate chips

This recipe is ridiculously easy and makes out-of-this-world delicious brownies. They come out super moist and fudgy, with that thin layer of classic brownie crispiness on top. They really turned out amazing and I loved the addition of quinoa to this original sweet treat.

Preheat oven to 350°F and grease a square baking dish. In a medium-sized saucepan on medium heat, heat coconut oil and add quinoa. Stir quinoa frequently until all quinoa has popped, then transfer to a large bowl. Add to mixing bowl flour, sugar, salt, cocoa powder, and baking powder; mix until combined.

   In another mixing bowl, combine liquid ingredients, water, brown sugar, maple syrup, vanilla, and melted butter. Add wet ingredients to dry ingredients then fold in chocolate chips. Spread batter evenly in greased baking dish. Bake for 30–35 minutes or until a toothpick comes out cleanly. Allow to cool and cut into 12 pieces.

Tip: Feel free to fold in some walnuts or pecans alongside the chocolate chips to give this dessert some versatility and extra oomph when you make it the second time.

QUINOA CANDY CLUSTERS

Makes about 2 dozen clusters

1 tablespoon coconut oil

¼ cup dry quinoa

½ cup peanut butter

¼ cup pure maple syrup

¼ cup toasted
   almonds, chopped

½ cup vegan chocolate chips

2 tablespoons vegan milk

My all-time favorite desserts are the ones that come together easily (particularly no-bake recipes) and taste incredibly amazing. These candy clusters will impress your guests and leave them guessing about the popped quinoa in them, which resemble the crispiness in other similar candies yet holds precious protein and amino acids that other candies cannot even touch.

Line a large baking sheet with parchment paper. In a medium-sized saucepan on medium heat, heat coconut oil and add quinoa. Stir quinoa frequently until all quinoa has popped, transfer to a mixing bowl to cool. Add to mixing bowl peanut butter, maple syrup and almonds and combine.

Grab candy mixture into clusters and set on parchment; chill in the refrigerator for 30 minutes. Melt together chocolate chips and milk and coat the candy clusters with this chocolate. Set on the parchment paper and refrigerate until the chocolate coating has hardened.

Tip: Try using sunflower seed butter or cashew butter instead of peanut butter or else incorporate different mix-ins like shredded coconut, mini chocolate chips, pecans, mini marshmallows, dried fruits or whatever you like.

QUINOA PECAN PIE

Serves 6–8

1 cup cooked
 quinoa, any type

1½ cups pecan halves

1 cup brown sugar

½ cup brown rice syrup

¼ teaspoon sea salt

1 (9-inch) prepared graham
 cracker pie crust

Pecan pie is one of the greatest of delicacies, so it was only natural I'd want to make a healthier version (and a way easier one too!) including quinoa for this book. You will love the rich flavors and nuttiness of this pie.

Preheat oven to 375°F. In a large mixing bowl, combine quinoa, pecans, sugar, syrup and salt, transfer to pie crust. Bake for 40–45 minutes. Cool and refrigerate for 1–2 hours before serving.

Tip: This dish can be served with a dollop of vegan whipped topping atop each slice of pie or a la mode with a generous scoop of your favorite ice cream on top. Vanilla, coffee, or caramel ice cream tastes amazing with this pie.

QUINOA MACAROONS

Makes about 2 dozen cookies

1 tablespoon coconut oil

¼ cup dry quinoa

1 (14-ounce) bag coconut, shredded and sweetened

¾ cup brown rice syrup

3 tablespoons coconut flour

¼ teaspoon sea salt

Macaroons, not be mistaken for macarons, are delightful little coconut cookies. Now with the inclusion of quinoa, these are twice as delightful!

Preheat oven to 325°F and line a large baking sheet with parchment paper. In a medium-sized saucepan on medium heat, heat coconut oil and add quinoa. Stir quinoa frequently until all quinoa has popped, then transfer to a large mixing bowl to cool.

Add to the mixing bowl shredded coconut, brown rice syrup, coconut flour and salt and combine. Roll cookie dough into balls. Bake for 20–25 minutes or until cookies are lightly golden brown.

Tip: Drizzle melted chocolate on top of these macaroon cookies or dip half the cookie in melted chocolate for a tasty treat and a gorgeous presentation.

POPPED QUINOA POPCORN BALLS

Serves 10

1 tablespoon coconut oil

¼ cup dry quinoa

4 quarts popcorn, popped

¾ cup cane sugar

½ cup brown rice syrup

⅛ cup water

⅛ teaspoon sea salt

1½ tablespoons vegan butter

½ teaspoon pure
   vanilla extract

I grew up in the late 1980s and early 1990s and distinctly recall eating way too many popcorn balls in the autumn, especially around Halloween time. Now with the addition of popped quinoa, they are as healthful as they are guaranteed to stick in your teeth! Make these in the fall, or any time of the year.

Line a large baking sheet with parchment paper. In a medium-sized saucepan on medium heat, heat coconut oil and add quinoa. Stir quinoa frequently until all quinoa has popped, transfer to a large mixing bowl to cool; combine with popcorn.

In a large saucepan on medium heat, combine sugar, brown rice syrup, water, and salt until "soft-ball stage" is reached (about 235°F on a candy thermometer). Remove from the heat and add vegan butter, vanilla. Pour over quinoa and popcorn mixture and mix until it is evenly coated. Allow to cool enough to safely handle, then shape into balls about 3 inches in size. Allow to cool and they will harden and set.

Tip: During the final mixing stage, you can add fun mix-ins like sprinkles to match whatever occasion or season you are serving these for. Use an all-natural wax paper or parchment paper to wrap the popcorn ball.

POPPED QUINOA CUPS

Serves 10–12

1 tablespoon coconut oil

¼ cup dry quinoa

½ cup brown rice syrup

1 cup mixed nuts, chopped

¼ cup raisins, chopped

⅓ cup chocolate chips

1 tablespoon vegan milk

These sweet treats are a sort of nougat-like candy cup coated in chocolate. They remind me almost of peanut butter cups without the peanuts; they have an old timey, old-fashioned quality about them. It is hard to explain, really, but these candies have a vibe all their own. You will just have to make them to see!

Line two muffin pans with paper liners. In a medium-sized saucepan on medium heat, heat coconut oil and add quinoa. Stir quinoa frequently until all quinoa has popped and transfer to a bowl to cool.

Once cooled, add brown rice syrup, mixed nuts, and raisins; transfer to muffin cups and press down. Melt chocolate chips and milk then spread on top of candy cups or drizzle chocolate, depending on preference. Allow to set in refrigerator for 1 hour before serving.

Tip: Play around with different mix-ins for these cups. You can add in shredded coconut instead of raisins or add in mini chocolate or peanut butter chips, too!

POPPED QUINOA CANDY BARS

Makes 10 candy bars

1 tablespoon coconut oil

¼ cup dry quinoa

½ cup almond butter

¾ cup peanut butter, creamy

½ cup powdered sugar

2 tablespoons
   coconut, shredded

2 tablespoons
   walnuts, chopped

⅛ teaspoon sea salt

½ cup chocolate chips

2 tablespoons vegan milk

¼ teaspoon pure
   vanilla extract

Every time I make a homemade candy bar, I am reminded of why I prefer making my own over the store-bought kind. These candy bars just taste way fresher since they have not been sitting in a wrapper on the grocery store shelf for who knows how long. Even the walnuts taste nice and fresh. Consider using different types of nuts for variation or to make different styles of candy bar to jazz up your dessert tray.

Line a large baking sheet with parchment paper. In a medium-sized saucepan on medium heat, heat coconut oil and add quinoa. Stir quinoa frequently until all quinoa has popped and transfer to a bowl to cool. Once cooled, add almond butter, peanut butter, powdered sugar, coconut, walnuts, and salt. Form into logs and arrange on baking sheet; place in freezer until ready to dip in chocolate coating.

To make chocolate candy coating, melt chocolate chips, milk, and vanilla in a medium-sized saucepan, stirring constantly. Remove from heat and carefully dip each candy bar into chocolate and place back on parchment paper to set. Let set in the refrigerator.

Tip: These candy bars are best stored in an airtight container in the refrigerator, especially during warmer months or if the temperature in your home is warm—these *can* get melty.

POPPED QUINOA LAYER COOKIES

Makes 18–20 servings

1 tablespoon coconut oil

¼ cup dry quinoa

½ cup vegan butter, melted

1 cup graham
    crackers, crumbled

1 (14-ounce) can vegan
    condensed milk

1 cup vegan chocolate chips

1½ cups coconut, flaked
    or shredded

1 cup walnuts, chopped

I have such fond memories of enjoying these cookies when I was a child, especially around the holidays... though these cookies make the perfect all year round sweet treat! These days, I like to bake them any time and enjoy them no matter the season.

Preheat oven to 350°F and grease a 9 x 13-inch baking dish. In a medium-sized saucepan on medium heat, heat coconut oil and add quinoa. Stir quinoa frequently until all quinoa has popped and remove from heat. In a large mixing bowl, combine popped quinoa, graham cracker crumbles and melted butter; mix well until combined. Press quinoa cracker mixture into the bottom of the baking dish to create the first layer. Continue to add layers, spreading evenly vegan condensed milk, chocolate chips, coconut, and nuts then press down using a large spatula. Bake for 25 minutes or until tops begin to turn lightly brown. Allow cookies to cool just enough to safely handle, then cut into squares.

Tip: The invention of vegan condensed milk has made recipes like these layer cookies so much simpler. I have been able to find this condensed milk everywhere from grocery stores to health food stores; however, if you cannot find this prepared milk readily available to you, it is easy to make your own at home with four to five simple ingredients (some recipes being cashews, powdered soy milk, sugar, water and coconut oil blended then reduced down).

POPPED QUINOA ALMOND BARK CANDY

Serves 12–15

1 tablespoon extra-virgin olive oil

¼ cup dry quinoa

3 cups vegan chocolate chips

2 tablespoons coconut oil

2 tablespoons pure maple syrup

1 teaspoon vegan milk

¼ teaspoon almond extract

¼ teaspoon pure vanilla extract

½ cup slivered almonds

2 teaspoons coarse sea salt

For years, vegans went without candy like this. No longer! We have all the culinary products we need available to us and the knowledge needed to make our own ingredients. We can even add popped quinoa to our bark candies just to show off!

In a medium-sized saucepan on medium heat, heat olive oil and add quinoa. Stir quinoa frequently until all quinoa has popped and transfer to a bowl to cool and set aside. Line a medium baking sheet with parchment paper.

Then, in a large saucepan, combine chocolate chips, coconut oil, maple syrup, milk, almond and vanilla extracts, stir constantly until melted and well-combined. Quickly transfer chocolate mixture to the lined baking sheet, spread evenly then top with almonds and sea salt.

Allow to cool and set in refrigerator, for about an hour or longer. Once set, break up into pieces of various shapes and sizes.

Tip: You can wrap candy bark pieces in waxed paper and store in the refrigerator for about one week.

POPPED QUINOA NUT BUTTER CUPS

Makes 36 nut butter cups

1 tablespoon extra-virgin
  olive oil

¼ cup dry quinoa

1 cup nut butter, creamy

¼ cup vegan butter, softened

½ cup powdered sugar

¼ teaspoon sea salt

3 cups vegan
  chocolate chips

This is a great recipe for the nut butter lover in anyone. You can use any nut or seed butter you would like in this dessert. I have made this with any and all of them and can confidently say that they all work really well. You can even make a few different kinds and serve them up for your next gathering.

In a medium-sized saucepan on medium heat, heat olive oil and add quinoa. Stir quinoa frequently until all quinoa has popped and transfer to a bowl to cool and set aside. In a medium mixing bowl, combine ½ cup nut butter, half of the popped quinoa, vegan butter, powdered sugar, and salt; cover and refrigerate.

In a medium saucepan on low heat, melt together remaining ½ cup nut butter, chocolate chips and remaining popped quinoa. Remove from heat and set aside. Divide nut butter mixture into 36 balls. Pour melted chocolate into 36 mini muffin cup liners, filling about ⅓ of the cup, then drop a nut butter ball into each cup, pressing down into the chocolate. Pour the remaining chocolate evenly into each cup, covering the nut butter filling. Refrigerate for at least several hours before enjoying (though overnight is best).

Tip: To make these nut butter cups more festive for specific occasions, during the final step of pouring chocolate on top, sprinkle some sparkly sugar or candy sprinkles on top.

QUINOA JAM THUMBPRINT COOKIES

Serves 18–20

2 cups all-purpose flour

¼ teaspoon ground
   cinnamon

¼ teaspoon salt

½ cup cane sugar

¾ cup vegan butter, softened

2 tablespoons vegan milk

1 teaspoon vanilla extract

¼ teaspoon almond extract

⅓ cup fruit preserves or
   vegan jam

A recipe like this is wonderful because you can fill the well in the thumbprint cookies with any flavor of fruit preserves or different flavors of jam to make a beautiful cookie tray that is sure to turn heads at your next neighborhood cookie swap. Aren't customizable recipes just the best?

Preheat oven to 350°F and line two large baking sheets with parchment paper. In a large mixing bowl, combine flour, cinnamon and salt, then add sugar. Cut in vegan butter, then slowly add vegan milk, vanilla, and almond extracts. On a floured surface, gently knead dough, then roll into balls. Place each ball on parchment lined baking sheets and press your thumb down to make an indent or small well. Fill with preserves or jam.

Bake for 10–15 minutes or until cookies are very lightly golden.

Tip: When kneading the dough, if it seems dry or like it needs more liquid, add a little water to it.

APPLE QUINOA STRUDEL

Serves 4–6

3 apples, thinly sliced

½ cup cooked
quinoa, any type

1 cup brown sugar

½ cup golden raisins

½ teaspoon cinnamon

¼ cup walnuts or
pecans, chopped

1 sheet frozen puff
pastry, thawed

3 tablespoons vegan
butter, melted

1 tablespoon cane sugar

Strudel only *seems* like a complicated dish to make, but I promise it's not. By using puff pastry in this recipe, this dessert looks much fancier than its easy preparation would lead you to believe. It will certainly impress!

Preheat oven to 400°F and line a large baking sheet with parchment paper. In a large mixing bowl, toss apples, cooked quinoa, brown sugar, raisins, cinnamon, and nuts. Transfer to the middle of the puff pastry on the baking sheet and fold the pastry dough sides inward.

Seal the middle by pressing with your fingers, adding water if needed. Make a few slits in the dough to vent, then brush the top of the dough with melted butter and sprinkle with sugar.

Bake for 30–35 minutes, or until golden brown in color and the puff pastry is cooked thoroughly.

Tip: This strudel tastes awesome with a dollop of vegan whipped topping or a la mode with a nice heaping scoop of vanilla ice cream!

QUINOA CAKE POPS

Serves 15–20

2 cups all-purpose flour

1½ cups cane sugar

¾ cup cocoa powder

1 teaspoon baking soda

2 teaspoons baking powder

½ teaspoon salt

1 cup vegan milk

½ vegan butter, melted

1 tablespoon pure vanilla extract

1 ripe banana, mashed

½ cup water

½ cup vegetable shortening

4 cups powdered sugar

1 tablespoon extra-virgin olive oil

¼ cup dry quinoa

½ cup vegan chocolate chips

1 tablespoon coconut oil

15–20 cake pop sticks

What I love most about this recipe is that quinoa is used two ways—both in the flour and popped on the outside of the cake. People may initially think these cake pops are a little strange with quinoa on the chocolate outer coating, but once they give them a taste, they will never question your judgement again.

Preheat oven to 350°F and grease a 9 x 13-inch baking dish. In a large mixing bowl, combine flour, sugar, cocoa powder, baking soda, baking powder, salt, milk, butter, vanilla, banana, and water; transfer batter to greased baking pan and bake for 40 minutes or until a cake checker comes out cleanly.

Once cool, fluff cake with a fork to make crumbles. Beat vegetable shortening and powdered sugar and mix into cake crumbles. Make and roll balls about 2 inches in diameter out of the cake mixture and transfer to a parchment lined baking sheet. Freeze until ready to dip in coating.

In a medium-sized saucepan on medium heat, heat olive oil and add quinoa. Stir quinoa frequently until all quinoa has popped and transfer to a bowl to cool. Melt chocolate chips and coconut oil to make cake pop coating.

Take a cake pop stick, dip it into the chocolate coating and then into the cake ball, before returning to baking sheet. Do this for each cake pop to allow the sticks to set into the cake pops. Take each cake pop, dip into chocolate coating, and roll into popped quinoa. Allow to set on baking sheet in refrigerator.

Tip: Use all-natural food coloring to make popped quinoa more festive! For example, you can divide popped quinoa into two bowls, coloring one red and the other green, for Christmas holiday popped quinoa.

QUINOA PUMPKIN CHEESECAKE CUPS

Serves 6

1 package refrigerated
   vegan pie crust, cut
   into 6 rounds

½ cup canned
   pumpkin puree

¼ cup firm tofu, drained

¼ cup cane sugar

½ teaspoon pure
   vanilla extract

2 tablespoons all-
   purpose flour

¼ teaspoon baking powder

½ teaspoon
   ground cinnamon

⅛ teaspoon sea salt

¼ cup cooked
   quinoa, any type

I love these petite cheesecake cups during fall time, but they are a nice treat to enjoy any day of the year, no matter the season. These are so stinking cute that your guests will be thrilled to have one of these on their plate after dinner!

Preheat oven to 350°F. Lightly grease six muffin tin spots and gently press dough into them. In a blender or food processor, blend pumpkin, tofu, sugar, vanilla, flour, baking powder, cinnamon, and salt; transfer to a mixing bowl and fold in cooked quinoa. Evenly distribute cheesecake filling to each of the six muffin cups.

Bake for 20 miwnutes or until cheesecake is firm and crust is golden and well-done. Allow to cool for at least 20 minutes then cover and refrigerate cheesecake cups for 4 hours before serving.

Tip: Serve on cute plates with a nice dollop of vegan whipped topping and a little scoop of ice cream right on top. You can even garnish with a sprig of mint, if desired.

PEANUT CHOCOLATE QUINOA CLUSTERS

Makes 1 dozen clusters

1 tablespoon extra-virgin
    olive oil

¼ cup dry quinoa

2 tablespoons coconut oil

2 cups vegan
    chocolate chips

½ cup roasted peanuts

⅛ teaspoon sea salt

Out of all the flavor combinations in the world, peanuts and chocolate seem to go together the absolute best. For candy and desserts like this one, I always prefer to have something with nuts in it to get the most out of my calories and get in that protein and those healthy fats. Popped quinoa being the star of this candy alongside these delicious flavors of chocolate and peanuts, it just works amazingly.

Line a large baking sheet with parchment paper and set aside. In a medium-sized saucepan on medium heat, heat olive oil and add quinoa. Stir quinoa frequently until all quinoa has popped and transfer to a bowl to cool and set aside. In a medium saucepan, melt coconut oil and chocolate together then mix peanuts and sea salt; remove from heat.

Allow the mixture to begin to cool, stirring often, until it reaches a workable consistency. Add popped quinoa to the mixture, form into clusters and place onto the baking sheet. Allow to chill in the refrigerator for 30 minutes before serving.

Tip: You can use nuts or mix-ins other than peanuts in this recipe. Colored sprinkles can also be added for fun.

SWEET QUINOA LEMON TARTS

Makes 2 dozen tarts

1 ½ cups all-purpose flour

½ teaspoon baking soda

¼ teaspoon baking powder

½ cup vegan butter, softened

¾ cup cane sugar

½ teaspoon pure
vanilla extract

1 ½ cups vegan lemon curd

¼ cup cooked
quinoa, any type

The perfect dessert for when you want a bite of something petite and sweet—nothing too heavy like cake or brownies. These are the perfect dessert to enjoy with tea or bring along with you on an afternoon picnic in the park. The lemon is refreshing and appetizing while the quinoa pairs with it nicely while adding protein, amino acids, and minerals to your dessert.

Preheat oven to 375°F and grease a mini muffin pan. In a small bowl, combine flour, baking soda, and baking powder, then cream in butter, sugar, and vanilla. Divide dough into 24 dough balls; push a ball into each greased mini muffin cup. Bake for 8–10 minutes or until tart cups are cooked and lightly browned but not overcooked.

Allow to cool completely before filling each tart cup with lemon curd mixture, which is mixing lemon curd and cooked quinoa together. Allow tarts to chill for several hours or overnight.

Tip: Vegan lemon curd is readily available now in supermarkets, natural food stores and online, but if you cannot find it, try making your own and storing it in a mason jar in your refrigerator.

CHOCOLATE COVERED STRAWBERRIES

WITH VANILLA POPPED QUINOA

Serves 4–6

1 tablespoon extra-virgin olive oil

½ teaspoon pure vanilla extract

¼ cup dry quinoa

1 pound fresh strawberries, washed and stems removed

1 tablespoon coconut oil

2 cups vegan chocolate chips

2 teaspoons vegan milk

Any time you have chocolate and fresh ripe strawberries on hand, you should be making chocolate covered strawberries. It's a no brainer! And with the inclusion of vanilla flavored popped quinoa to coat them, you'll be getting a mouthful of flavors and textures that you will love! Plus, how can you go wrong with fresh fruit, protein-packed quinoa, and antioxidant rich chocolate? Hard to believe this is a dessert!

In a medium-sized saucepan on medium heat, heat olive oil, vanilla extract and add quinoa. Stir quinoa frequently until all quinoa has popped and transfer to a bowl to cool and set aside. In a small saucepan on low heat, melt together coconut oil, chocolate chips and milk.

Line a large baking sheet with parchment paper. Dip each strawberry in chocolate mixture, roll into popped quinoa, and place on baking sheet. Refrigerate for 30 minutes.

Tip: These sweet treats are wonderful to make for Valentine's Day or other special holidays.

CHOCOLATE COVERED COCONUT QUINOA BARS

Serves 12

½ cup cooked
   quinoa, any type

1½ cups coconut, shredded

¼ teaspoon pure
   vanilla extract

¼ teaspoon sea salt

½ cup pure maple syrup

2 cups vegan
   chocolate chips

1 tablespoon coconut oil

1 tablespoon vegan milk

These are one of the easiest-to-prepare candies that I have ever made. These candy bars just might remind you of a familiar flavor, too…except that they are much healthier thanks to the superfood that is quinoa.

Line a large baking sheet with parchment paper. In a medium mixing bowl, combine cooked quinoa, coconut, vanilla, salt, and maple syrup; form into a ball then refrigerate. In a medium saucepan on low heat, melt chocolate chips, coconut oil and milk, stirring constantly until melty and well combined.

Remove from heat and form quinoa coconut mixture into 12 bars. Dip into chocolate and return to the parchment lined baking sheet to set. Refrigerate for 30 minutes or until chocolate coating has hardened.

Tip: To add an extra-special finishing touch to these candy bars, after forming the quinoa coconut logs, press an almond into the tops and coat with chocolate.

EASY ROCKY ROAD QUINOA CANDIES
Serves 6–8

1 tablespoon extra-virgin olive oil

½ teaspoon pure vanilla extract

¼ cup dry quinoa

1 tablespoon coconut oil

2 cups vegan chocolate chips

2 teaspoons vegan milk

½ cup walnuts, chopped

¼ cup almonds, chopped

½ cup vegan mini marshmallows

The only problem with these candies is that each time I make them, I can't stop eating them! They have the perfect balance of sweet, savory and crunchy while offering the classic rocky road style that we all know and love. This dessert also has a cool retro vibe since these candies remind me so much of old fashioned ones. I cannot resist them, and I think you'll love them, too!

In a medium-sized saucepan on medium heat, heat olive oil, vanilla extract and add quinoa. Stir quinoa frequently until all quinoa has popped and transfer to a bowl to cool and set aside. In a small saucepan on low heat, melt together coconut oil, chocolate chips and milk. Remove from heat and fold in popped quinoa, walnuts, almonds, and vegan marshmallows.

Line a large baking sheet with parchment paper. Using a spoon, drop candy mixture into piles on the baking sheet (you can use the spoon to form them and make them neater or else keep them as clusters) and transfer to freezer immediately. Allow to set for 1 hour in freezer.

Tip: These can be stored in an airtight container in the refrigerator for up to one week. If you have trouble finding vegan mini marshmallows and can only find the larger sized ones, simply chop them into smaller pieces for use in this recipe.

QUINOA FRUIT TEA CAKE LOAF

Serves 8–10

- 1 tablespoon extra-virgin olive oil
- ¼ cup dry quinoa
- 1 cup English breakfast tea, strongly brewed or 1 cup boiled water
- 1 cup mixed dried fruit
- ½ cup cane sugar
- 1 tablespoon jam or preserves, any flavor
- 1 cup all-purpose flour
- 2 teaspoons baking powder
- 1 teaspoon ground cinnamon
- 2 tablespoons water

Yes, there *is* a fruit cake in this book. But given that this one is English and has tea in it, it's not exactly like the classic fruit cake that everyone gives a hard time. Note that if you are planning on serving this loaf to people who are non-adults or are caffeine sensitive, use herbal tea or just plump up the dried fruit using boiled water. When I make this in the morning for overnight guests, I always soak my dried fruits in water so that everyone can enjoy it (and you can always serve the cake loaf slices alongside a cup of English tea—it's quite the pairing!

Preheat oven to 350°F and grease a loaf pan. Soak dried fruit in tea while preparing the rest of the recipe. In a medium-sized saucepan on medium heat, heat olive oil and add quinoa. Stir quinoa frequently until all quinoa has popped and transfer to a large mixing bowl; combine fruit and tea mixture, sugar, jam, flour, baking powder, cinnamon, and water. Transfer batter to greased loaf pan and bake for 60 minutes or until cake tester comes out cleanly. Allow to cool for 20–30 minutes before removing from pan.

Tip: You will like this one, trust me. Just serve it buttered like you would serve a slice of pumpkin loaf. I like to use California raisins, golden raisins, and dried cranberries in mine, but the possibilities are endless with the number of delicious dried fruits available.

MINI QUINOA TRIFLE DESSERT CUPS

Serves 4

4 cups vegan
   whipped topping

2 cups cooked
   quinoa, any type

1½ cups vegan cake
   crumbles, chocolate
   or vanilla

4 tablespoons
   chocolate syrup

4 maraschino cherries

If you are looking for a distinctive and elegant dessert to serve to your guests during your next dinner party, a trifle is the way to go. With little effort, you can serve up a sweet end to the meal that looks truly worthy of being served at a five-star restaurant.

In four serving cups, arrange trifle layers in this order: whipped topping, quinoa, cake crumbles and chocolate syrup, ending with the last layer being whipped topping. Garnish each cup with a cherry.

Tip: Your mini trifle cups make a difference! Serve this dessert in a cup that matches the theme or aesthetic of the occasion or event. You can go more casual if it is a laidback get together or go fancy with your trifle glassware for more formal events.

QUINOA BUTTER COOKIES

Makes about 30 cookies

1 tablespoon extra-virgin olive oil

¼ cup dry quinoa

1 cup butter

1 cup cane sugar

2⅔ cups all-purpose flour

¼ teaspoon salt

1 teaspoon vanilla extract

Popped quinoa works so well in these butter cookies that upon trying them, I wondered why they'd ever been made without them!

Preheat an oven to 400°F and gather two large baking sheets, ungreased. In a medium-sized saucepan on medium heat, heat olive oil and add quinoa. Stir quinoa frequently until all quinoa has popped and transfer to a bowl to cool and set aside. Cream butter and sugar then add flour, salt, vanilla extract, and fold in popped quinoa.

On a lightly floured surface, gently knead the dough, then roll into a large log shape in plastic wrap or parchment paper. Refrigerate for 1–2 hours. When ready to bake, slice into half-inch slices and arrange 1 inch apart on the ungreased baking sheet. Bake for about 10 minutes or until cookies are slightly golden brown at the edges.

Tip: This dough can be kept and stored in refrigerator for up to one week until ready to use. It is a great idea to make this dough ahead of time for when company comes and you want to just pop a few cookies into the oven or toaster oven. This dough can also be frozen the same way, rolled into plastic wrap and placed in a freezer bag for up to one month. While you can use this butter cookie dough in a cookie press, please be aware that your cookies will come out thinner and take less time to bake. When using a cookie press, check the cookies around 7–8 minutes into baking.

QUINOA PEANUT BUTTER SQUARES

Serves 10

1 tablespoon coconut oil

¼ cup dry quinoa

1 cup peanut butter, creamy or chunky

½ cup powdered sugar

⅛ teaspoon sea salt

I wanted to do something with popped quinoa that reminded me of peanut butter fudge but make it healthy. These came out phenomenal! I also love that these are a no-bake dessert; the only real effort being made here is popping the quinoa, which is a breeze and takes nearly no time at all.

Line a medium-sized baking dish with parchment paper. In a medium-sized saucepan on medium heat, heat coconut oil and add quinoa. Stir quinoa frequently until all quinoa has popped and transfer to a bowl to cool. Once cooled, add peanut butter, powdered sugar, and salt to popped quinoa, and mix well. Press mixture into parchment-lined baking pan and spread evenly. Refrigerate for several hours until set, then cut into bite-sized squares.

Tip: Serve these on little foil or paper mini cupcake liners for an elegant look. You can match the liners with the holiday or occasion; if you are taking these to a baby shower (or hosting one) for instance, consider using pastel liners that are yellow, pink, or blue. Pastel liners are great for serving these treats to guests in the springtime.

QUINOA BAKLAVA

Makes 2 dozen baklava squares

1 tablespoon extra-virgin olive oil

¼ cup dry quinoa

3 cups walnuts, chopped

½ teaspoon pure vanilla extract

1 teaspoon ground cinnamon

1 cup vegan butter, melted

1 cup pure maple syrup

1 (16-ounce) package vegan phyllo dough

Tip: Make these baklava squares for friends and family. You may or may not want to tell them how easy it was to make; it depends on whether you want to keep them in a state of amazement and awe that you prepared this "complicated" dessert for them!

The assumption everyone always makes is that baklava is too difficult or too complicated to make. I recall a time when some friends and I were eating at a vegan pizzeria that served baklava for dessert, and all my friends agreed that they could only *wish* they knew how to make baklava. News flash: it is *not* hard to make! This is my even easier, super-simplified and quinoa-included version of vegan baklava.

Preheat oven to 350°F and grease a 9 x 13-inch baking dish. In a medium-sized saucepan on medium heat, heat olive oil and add quinoa. Stir quinoa frequently until all quinoa has popped and transfer to a large mixing bowl; combine with walnuts, vanilla, and cinnamon.

In a baking dish, prepare a good baklava base by laying down four phyllo sheets. Brush melted butter onto every other layer of the phyllo dough, then spread about one-third of the popped quinoa and walnut mixture evenly over the dough. Drizzle some of the maple syrup and repeat until all ingredients are used up. The last layer should be like the first, with four layers of phyllo, butter on every other layer. Using a sharp knife, cut baklava into 24 squares then bake for 25–30 minutes, or until baklava is golden and crisp.

SIMPLE POPPED QUINOA TRUFFLES

Serves 8–10

1 tablespoon extra-virgin olive oil

¼ cup dry quinoa

½ cup canned coconut milk

1 cup vegan chocolate chips

¼ teaspoon tsp vanilla extract

¼ cup cocoa powder for coating (optional)

These simple yet uber-flavorful truffles will knock your socks off! Plus, they are so easy to make—whip up a batch in mere minutes and be prepared to dazzle your guests or family members with this sweet dessert.

Line a large baking sheet with parchment paper and set aside. In a medium-sized saucepan on medium heat, heat olive oil and add quinoa. Stir quinoa frequently until all quinoa has popped and transfer to a large mixing bowl.

In a small saucepan, bring coconut milk to a boil and add to the popped quinoa; quickly add chocolate chips and vanilla, then stir and allow to sit for a few minutes to melt the chocolate. Stir occasionally as you allow the chocolate mixture to cool. Once fudgy, use a melon baller or tablespoon sized measuring spoon to scoop the truffles, roll in cocoa powder (if using), and place them onto the baking sheet. Allow to set in refrigerator for 1–2 hours before enjoying.

Tip: Can be stored in an airtight container in the refrigerator for up to one week.

QUINOA PINEAPPLE UPSIDE DOWN CAKE

Serves 10–12

1 tablespoon extra-virgin olive oil

¼ cup dry quinoa

1 box yellow cake mix

2 tablespoons brown sugar

1 (20-ounce) can pineapple rings, drained

1 (20-ounce) can cherry pie filling

½ cup vegan butter, melted

In creating this book, I considered requests from the two different sides of my readership. One group of people seem to be all about the vegan processed food and easy-to-make stuff; for these people, the more store bought ingredients used and the simpler it is to prepare, the better. The other group is all about natural every-thing! Make everything from scratch, even if it takes you hours. I am somewhere in between; as a chef, I do like to make my own creations solely from scratch when possible, but I am also a human who has to give myself a break sometimes and go with whatever is easiest, especially when I find myself super swamped with work and family life. This book is for everyone…but this recipe is definitely for my processed folks. We use boxed cake mix in this one, with all-natural or gluten-free organic cake mixes being preferred.

Preheat oven to 350°F and grease a 9-inch round cakepan. In a medium-sized saucepan on medium heat, heat olive oil and add quinoa. Stir quinoa frequently until all quinoa has popped and transfer to a large mixing bowl; combine with cake mix.

In the greased cake pan, sprinkle brown sugar, then place pineapple rings down in pan and add cherry pie filling on top of pineapples. Add cake mix and popped quinoa mixture, then pour on melted butter. Bake for 55–60 minutes or until cake appears to be shrinking away from sides of cake pan and cake is firm. Cake will be sticky, so when checking for doneness with a cake checker, keep that in mind. Allow cake to fully cool before removing from pan.

Tip: You can also use a Bundt cake pan for this recipe, which makes for a beautiful dessert look. I usually stick with the flat top, plain and ordinary looking Bundt pans for upside down cakes because the pineapples and cherries glazed are on the top, which is where all the beauty in this dish comes from. Consider adding pecans or walnuts to the topping or folded right into your cake!

QUINOA FUDGE SQUARES

Makes about 2 dozen squares

- 1 tablespoon extra-virgin olive oil
- ¼ cup dry quinoa
- 1 cup cashew butter, room temperature
- ⅓ cup coconut oil, melted
- ¼ cup cocoa powder
- ¼ cup pure maple syrup
- 1 teaspoon vanilla extract
- ¼ teaspoon sea salt

For a healthier take on fudge candy, try these fudge squares using protein and fiber-packed quinoa. These are so delicious that you will hardly even notice quinoa is included in the recipe list!

Grease a 9 x 13-inch baking pan and set aside. In a medium-sized saucepan on medium heat, heat olive oil and add quinoa. Stir quinoa frequently until all quinoa has popped and transfer to a bowl to cool and set aside. In a large mixing bowl or stand mixer, beat cashew butter, coconut oil, cocoa, maple syrup, vanilla, and sea salt. Fold in half the popped quinoa mixture. Press fudge into greased baking pan then evenly distribute remaining popped quinoa on top and lightly press down. Allow to set in freezer for one hour then cut into 24 squares.

Tip: These adorable fudge squares can be dressed up for holidays or occasions by pressing festive sprinkles on top along with the remaining popped quinoa during the final step. These fudge squares would look especially cute with orange and purple sprinkles during Halloween time, or pastel sprinkles during Easter. You can also serve these squares on small decorative mini muffin cups or dainty paper lace baker's doilies.

IN CLOSING

I HOPE THAT THIS book has sparked your imagination and inspired you to see quinoa in a whole new light. Whenever I write these cookbooks, I learn so much more about our culinary experiences as humans; how we are capable of doing so much and being ever so creative in seemingly unthinkable ways, so long as we believe in ourselves. Keep dreaming up wacky and weird food combinations using ingredients that society tells you "shouldn't really go together" because oftentimes they can and they do—this book is a testament to that!

We have learned so much together in these books. What quinoa is and where it came from, and the different types of quinoa available and how to prepare this super seed in many exciting and unique ways. We know how healthy adding quinoa into our daily lives is and also had a conversation about how to be responsible and aware when making purchases like quinoa. Let's not forget, after over one hundred recipes, we are, at the end of this book. I hope you enjoyed this quinoa adventure as much I did making it for you!

And for now, The Dirty Vegan is signing off. Happy cooking to you, my Friends.

Catherine Gill

Follow

@theDirtyVegan

theDirtyVegan_official

TheDirtyVegan

ACKNOWLEDGEMENTS

THERE ARE SO many people who have helped and inspired me, and who continue to do so throughout my holistic culinary journey. Thank you, from the bottom of my heart, to everyone who assisted in making this book and this beautiful vegan life possible. In no particular order, I would like to give the most heartfelt thanks to:

God…you know.

My daughter, S, who inspires me and who I am so proud of. You motivate me every second of every day to be the best version of myself. I wanted to also thank you for the contribution of your wonderful Quinwaffle recipe. Kiddos from around the globe will enjoy your recipe contributions with each book! You are such a great helper with all of my projects, and I appreciate and love you so much.

To my husband, J, thank you for all your help, hard work and dedication, and thank you for always encouraging my aspirations. You go above and beyond in helping me with these huge projects. I am grateful for your lovely photography, style, and artistic vision. I love and appreciate you.

Mom, you have inspired me to be a strong woman, to speak up for myself, and to be fearless. You need a special sort of confidence and strength to take on activism, to handle the sad parts of it. I would not be the person that I am today without you and Dad. Thank you for always working so hard to learn about vegan food over the years, and I am grateful for all of the vegan holidays that you have hosted and for all of the plant-based foods that you've learned to make for me! There is nothing greater than a mother's love.

Dad, thank you for helping me to see that animals are not food. I remember being a small child and noticing that you didn't want to eat meat that had bones or veins in it; that sparked the birth of a wise knowledge in me that has grown so much, and continues to do so. Thank you for encouraging me to learn more about the world and for passing on a wonderful passion for education. It is because of you and your cooking style that being in the kitchen is fun for me, and never feels like a job. I am so proud of you for becoming a vegetarian, though I am not surprised—you have always been a kind soul. Thank you for being the person I can talk with for hours about philosophy and other such intellectual (even hipster) things. Thanks to you and Mom, I am a woke individual who is fulfilling and exceeding my fiercest dreams.

To my brother, L, and my sister-in-law, T, I am so proud of you two for being healthcare workers during the tumultuous and devastating pandemic we faced. You both are so brave, hardworking, courageous, and selfless. L, I remember your words when the pandemic started, that you wanted to be there to help the people; you are a Helper. Those words will live in my heart forever and inspire me to contribute good to this world as well, just like you do. Thank you as well for always being my biggest cheerleader. You have been so supportive of my vegan lifestyle and have gotten so involved in the cause. Thank you for always going out of your way to prepare vegan meals at your home and to order vegan foods at all the events you and your family host; you do it not because you have to, but because you have a truly beautiful heart. You are my BFF, and I am always excited to tell you about my professional accomplishments. You are always so genuinely happy for me, and your faith and goodness inspire me to always be a person of virtue.

To D and R, thank you for all the support and encouragement you have given me throughout the years. The food chopper you gifted me for this project has been such a blessing and one of the kitchen gadgets I have been most thankful for. Lots of love and appreciation to you both!

To the amazing folks at Hatherleigh Press—my people, my team: Andrew Flach, Ryan Tumambing, Ryan Kennedy, Hannah Renouard, and the rest of the Hatherleigh family, thank you so much for all of your hard work and dedication. Thank you for believing in this project as much as I do, for believing in me, and for sharing my visions for this book and all our projects together. I value you and appreciate your trust in me. You made this possible. Thank you for helping me to check yet another dream off my list!

Most importantly, thank you to the animals, the "why I do what I do" in the vegan community and in social activism. I will never stop fighting for your freedom.

And thank you to the fans, readers, fellow activists and friends who have been working so bravely and selflessly to be voices for the animals. To my readers, especially those who have been reading my blog posts and articles since I first began writing and have been supporting my work and cookbooks for many years now—this is for you!

RECIPE INDEX

NOTES

NOTES